THE BUTLER AND TANNER STORY

BY

LORRAINE JOHNSON

FROME SOCIETY FOR LOCAL STUDY

MMXV

PUBLISHED BY

THE FROME SOCIETY FOR LOCAL STUDY

PRINTED FOR THINK DIGITAL BOOKS LTD

BY SHORT RUN PRESS LTD

©Lorraine Johnson

JUNE 2015

ISBN 978-0-9930605-0-2

'Pray stranger
that the forme be
resurrected
that's put to bed with
errors uncorrected'
[Inscription on gravestone of
Joseph Tanner, Printer
1928–2006]

Acknowledgements

There are many people to whom I owe a debt of gratitude for their generous assistance throughout the whole project. At Frome Heritage Museum I have been welcomed and helped enormously by Brian Marshall, Sue Bucklow and Jennie O'Kane and my heartfelt thanks go to them. In addition, Dr Emma Robinson and the rest of the committee have opened up new opportunities for me and I hope to make a positive contribution to the Museum over the coming years.

I am very grateful to Peter Clark and Alastair MacLeay of the Frome Society for Local Study for their tremendous support and enthusiasm for the venture. Thanks also go to Alan Yeates who has worked incredibly hard to produce such a well-designed book.

Thanks go to those former employees and directors who have made valid contributions to the work, including Emily Aston, Grant Aven, Mike Barnsley, David Bowden, Sally Bowden, Peter Branch, Steve Burry, Katrina Caffyn, Christian Coates, Clive Cook, Ryan Cook, Neville Dean, Joyce Dyer, Grant Evason, Jean Hicks, Mark Kempshall, Tom Larman, Marion Lucas, Simon Marks and Paul Veater.

A particular mention must be made of Mary Scott, a member of the Tanner family, who has been generous with her time and kindly provided some very interesting information.

Finally, thanks to Michael Richardson (Bristol University Library), Ian Leggett (Dennis Publishing) and Dan Brown (Bath Central Library) for their assistance.

Picture credits

All illustrations are from the Butler and Tanner archive in Frome Heritage Museum unless otherwise stated.

Picture credits: p. 10 (top) Alan Yeates; p. 12 Alan Yeates; p. 13 Sue Bucklow; p. 16 Alastair MacLeay; p. 36 Bath Central Library; p. 42 Sally Bowden; p. 43 (top) Steve Burry; p. 47 (bottom) Steve Burry; p. 50 Frome Society for Local Study; p. 60 Sally Bowden; p. 75 Steve Burry; p. 119 Sue Bucklow; p. 120 Sue Bucklow; p. 123 Neville Dean, p. 124 Neville Dean.

Contents

Preface

It is lamentable that the entire British printing trade has practically vanished over a matter of decades. The illustrious printing firm of Butler and Tanner in the town of Frome in Somerset has a long history which was, sadly, brought abruptly to a halt in 2014.

The aim of this book is to document the history of the firm so as to provide an insight into: the changing technologies, the personalities of those running the firm, the challenges posed to British businesses, and the role played by a town's substantial employer in its contribution to local society.

Using documentation from the Butler and Tanner archive and the testimonies of some of those associated with the firm, the purpose of this volume is to act as tribute to every single person who made a contribution to Butler and Tanner's proud history.

ONE

The Early Years of Printing in Frome

Portrait (in oils) of Abraham Crocker c.1800

When William Caxton established his press in the abbey precincts at Westminster, in 1476, he could never have imagined the significance that printing would subsequently obtain in England. Nor could he have envisaged the impact that his associated publishing and bookselling activities would have upon his homeland. He may, indeed, have been astonished had he known that a printing company in the town of Frome in Somerset, sending forth millions of volumes around the world, would be located on a road specifically named after him.

By the eighteenth century the printing trade was becoming well established throughout the English provinces where local printers would provide commercial printing services for customers within their immediate environs. Generally such trade would comprise broadsheets, advertising leaflets, posters and a whole host of ephemera catering for local businesses. Book printing would generally be limited to volumes produced largely on topics relevant to a local area and sold to a limited clientele.

Frome became home to a gentleman by the name of Abraham Crocker and it is believed that it was he who first established a printing firm within the town.[1] Having become a resident of Frome in 1783, taking on the role of Master

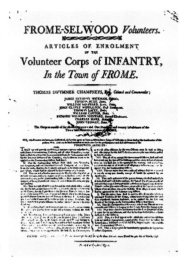

England had been at war with France since 1793: this broadsheet printed by Crocker in 1797 depicts the local response to such possible Napoleonic invasion

7

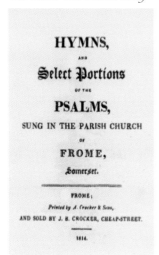

Title page of Crocker's hymn book printed in 1814

of the Bluecoat School, he appears to have printed his first item in 1797 in the form of a broadsheet. He had four sons: James who had established a bookshop and lending library in 7, Cheap Street in Frome by 1810; John who continued Abraham's printing undertakings at 7, Bath Street in Frome by 1815; Edmund whose artistic skills were harnessed by working as a map maker for the Ordnance Survey and Philip who illustrated the *History of Ancient Wiltshire*.[2] Abraham Crocker's book publications were typically themed volumes aimed at those locals who were both literate and wealthy enough to afford them.

A BRIEF
HISTORICAL ACCOUNT
OF
THE ALMSHOUSE AND SCHOOL
CHARITIES,
Within the Parish of Frome,
IN THE COUNTY OF
Somerset.

TO WHICH IS ADDED, AN APPENDIX,
RELATIVE TO
Mr. R. Stevens's Asylum and Hospital.

By A. CROCKER.

CROCKER and SONS, PRINTERS, BATH-STREET, FROME
1815.

Title page of a local history book written and printed by Crocker in 1815

Abraham Crocker retired in 1815 leaving James and John to run their respective sides of the business. However, with James' death in 1820 the bookselling business was sold to William Ponsford Penny who also acquired another book shop at 3, Bath Street in 1823 and moved the business from Cheap Street to the new premises. Following John Crocker's death in 1831, Penny purchased the printing side of the business from his widow in 1832 for £500.

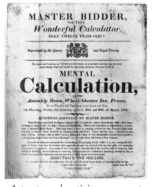

A poster advertising an event in the Wheat Sheaves public house in 1818

Following Penny's death in 1851 the firm's continuation was assured when his widow and two sons took over its running, renaming it W.C. & J. Penny.[3]

There was evidently enough printing business in the town to warrant more than one such enterprise for, quite separately in the same street in 1845, another small printing office was established. An outbuilding in Mansford's Yard (next to the *Wheat Sheaves* public house) which had, apparently, previously been used as stables, formed the modest premises now put to

William Langford

use as a print works. Initially set up for the chemist owner's printing needs, such as medicine labels and advertising leaflets for the latest pharmaceutical preparations, the press's output was soon expanded. The proprietor was William Langford who had acquired the double fronted chemist shop at 20, Bath Street, Frome around 1830.[4] Originally, not a local man, he had been apprenticed to a chemist named Butler, in High Wycombe. Butler's nephew, William Thomas Butler, was also articled to him at the same time and the two became good friends despite a three-year age gap. In 1844, Langford was joined by his childhood friend, who moved from Buckinghamshire to the West Country to become his business partner, the firm subsequently

William Thomas Butler

(and unsurprisingly) named Langford and Butler. It was this enterprise that became the forerunner of the Butler and Tanner partnership whose name was to become synonymous with printing in the town of Frome for well over a century.

The Wheat Sheaves Inn, the press would have been situated in the stables through the archway

Whilst Langford concentrated on his pharmaceutical occupation Butler devoted himself to the printing side of the business. It was on their presses that the first *Frome Almanack* was produced at the end of 1846 by the Langford and Butler partnership.[5] Just two years later Langford had retired from the printing side of the business and Butler was running it alone.[6] In 1853, William Butler moved the printing press to a new stone building at the end of his garden at Castle House, on the corner of Long Row (later renamed Castle Street) and Nail Street (later renamed Trinity Street) in the town, where he continued to develop the printing

William Butler's abode at Castle House, Frome

business. He called the enterprise, the Selwood Printing Office. The name was chosen in reference to Frome-Selwood, a former name for the town derived from Selwood Forest once covering large areas of Wiltshire and Somerset.[7] At that time the firm was fairly unremarkable; an example of a typical reasonably sized commercial printer of the type to be found in any substantial town across the country. An advertisement in the 1854 *Frome Almanack* printed by Butler and published by Langford, describes Butler's business as that of 'General Letterpress Printer'.

In 1855 William Langford sold the pharmacy, his share of the printing business and his

Printed advertisement for Randall's preparations

proprietorship of the *Somerset and Wilts. Journal*, a publication he had also founded.[8] William Thomas Butler, however, continued the printing business alone (employing two men and five boys) ensuring that the presses were kept busy, advertising the wide range of printing services he was able to provide: books on general literature; lectures; sermons, overseers' and parish works of all kinds; auction bills; catalogues; shop bills; circulars; prospectuses; bill heads; address cards etc.[9]

Around 1857 he purchased a small steam engine to power the press and renamed the business 'W.T. Butler's Steam Printing Works'. The recent railway connection from Frome to London (1850) may have offered Butler hopes of further expansion and hence the investment into the technology to

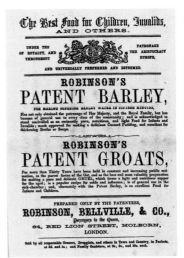

Printed advertisement for Robinson, Bellville and Co.'s patent barley and patent groats

allow faster production rates. Butler's print works was not only servicing the printing needs of local establishments, for by this time his customer base had expanded to as far afield as Brighton, Cardiff, Matlock in Derbyshire and across the Irish Sea to Dublin. His

Interior of the Selwood Printing Office c. 1863, showing the compositors setting type at their cases [left], the creation of the 'formes' [centre] and the letterpress machinery [right]

customers included Robinson's for their 'patent barley' and 'patent groats', Ferris of Bristol who were 'Chemists to Her Majesty', another royally connected customer – Joseph Gillot

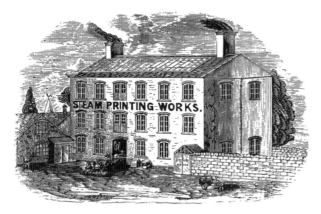

Steam Printing Works, Frome c. 1860

(metallic pen makers by 'Royal Command') – and A. Rowland and Sons, Hatton Gardens, manufacturers of the, then popular, 'Macassar Oil'.[10]

By September 1863 Butler was formally joined in partnership by Joseph Tanner, their combined business described as 'General Letter Press Printing and Stereotype Founding'.[11] The men had become acquainted through their association with the Zion Congregational Church in Whittox Lane.[12] In fact, Crocker, Langford, Butler and Tanner had all been members of the same church.

Born in 1835[13], the first son, following three daughters, Joseph (named after his father) Tanner was 28 years old by the time he joined ranks with Butler. Tanner's industrial experience had been gained in local cloth mills. It was the knowledge he had gained from witnessing failure to invest in technology and the trade's ultimate demise that was to stand

Butler and Tanner stone colophon, 1870

him in good stead. He realised that investment in the printing industry was vital in order to move forward and make the most of opportunities; an attitude that was maintained throughout the following generations of Tanners and one which would ensure the firm's ultimate success.

In true printing tradition, the firm of Butler and Tanner held an annual 'wayzgoose' for their workers; a practice started when the partnership was initiated in 1863. (Originally a wayzgoose referred to entertainment given by a master printer to his workmen each year on, or around, St Bartholomew's Day which is 24th August. It marked the traditional end of summer and the start of the season of working by candlelight. In more modern times, it came to refer to an annual outing and dinner for the staff of a printing works or the printers of a newspaper.) An existing printed itinerary shows the fairly elaborate nature of these excursions which must have provided really memorable occasions for everyone who participated. The summer of 1869 saw the workers from the Selwood Printing Works, boarding three carriages of a train from Frome to Weymouth for their sixth annual outing. Dinner was provided for them at the Victoria and Great Western Hotel and steam boats took them to Portland.[14]

Over the following years the partners, keen to expand the business, bought up a good deal of property in and around Blunt Street (later named Selwood Road) and Nail Street (later renamed Trinity Street), including several tenement cottages, dwelling houses, weaving shops, a chemist and druggist shop, a hat and cap manufacturer's shop and *The Ship* public house.[15] Once demolished, these properties allowed for a vast site, upon which an enormous factory was built. The combined partnership allowed the firm to expand their horizons wider than the local economy. Butler set up an office in Paternoster Row in London to allow him to concentrate on the sales side of the business, expressing a desire to live closer to the capital. In a formal agreement, the pair agreed a temporary arrangement (nine months) whereby he would be freed from his obligations and responsibilities of the business and that Joseph Tanner was to run the firm.[16]

The following year Butler agreed that Tanner be extended a commission of one per cent on the gross return of sales for the current year (1st July, 1866 to 30th June, 1867) because of 'giving extra services' and as he 'becomes a guarantee for the firm to the extent of £1,000'.[17] Joseph Tanner could certainly not be accused of being unambitious: plans included exhibiting at the Paris Exhibition in 1867 where examples of the firm's block and letterpress printing were awarded a bronze medal.[18]

Under the first four years of Joseph Tanner's control the works' output doubled. He invested in new machinery to speed up production and to be better able to produce high quality printing. Speedier production meant lower prices to both established local customers and for the new trade being brought in from

The bronze medal engraved with the firm's name

the London publishers. Expansion continued apace and the Selwood Printing Works (as it was now known), Frome was fast growing into a sizeable business. Indeed, a contemporary account of the firm [c. 1868] gives a clear indication of just how comprehensive a service the printers were able to provide by that stage:

> The Selwood Printing Works (proprietors: Messrs. Butler and Tanner) although one of the youngest, is among the most interesting establishments in town. There the visitor is enabled to trace the process by which an author's thoughts are sent forth to the world, from the moment the manuscript containing them is put into the hands of the type-setter, or compositor, to the time when, radiant in all the beauty of colour and gold, the volume is ready to be issued to the public.
>
> Suffice to say this Establishment is the largest printing office in the West of England, and combines in one building the various processes of printing, stereotyping and binding. It would be difficult to estimate the producing power of such an establishment as there is so much difference between printing and other industrial arts, and there are so many

matters connected with printing which would render any statistics we could give only approximations. We may state, however, that the firm employs upwards of 150 hands, and lies with the best London houses in the character and style of work produced. Amongst other productions may be noticed that marvel of cheapness the 'Penny Pilgrim's Progress' of which more than half a million copies have already been sold. Messrs Butler and Tanner are the printers of several monthly publications, among which may be mentioned the 'Sunday Teacher's Treasury', the 'Mother's Treasury' and 'Father William's Stories' some of which are tastefully illustrated. The printing machines in operation in this establishment are from famous makers in London and Scotland, and the types are from the best foundries in various parts of England. The large quantity of paper required for the business so extensive is supplied from mills east, west, north and south. The engine working the whole of the machinery was built by our townsman, Mr Haley; and the columnar chimney, which is one of the landmarks of the town, is also the design of a townsman, Mr Chapman.

The whole establishment is worthy of a visit, not only for its perfection, but as a novel branch of industry in the town; in times past, a printing office was not a thing unknown in Froome, but this must exceed its pre-decessors as a power-loom does a hand loom.[19]

THE SHRIMPERS.

An illustrated page from the Home Words magazine

In 1868, plans were put into place for the dissolution of the partnership, with Tanner agreeing to pay Butler half of the share of the business, thus making him sole proprietor.[20] By the January of 1869 the financial transactions had been put in force with Butler receiving the sum of £1,350 for a half interest in the factory. In addition, Tanner was to pay off a half of the existing debt which, it was agreed, was between £1,400 and £1,500. Whilst the partnership was to be dissolved on 30th June, 1868 the dissolution was not to be 'publicly advertised or notified' and that

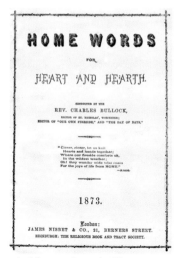

A title page from the Home Words magazine, printed in 1873

if Joseph Tanner were to die before 1878 that Butler could have first refusal of purchasing the business.[21] However, six years later a letter under seal cancelled claims from this agreement 'mutually terminates and put an end to the arrangements subsisting between us' and 'mutually release each other from all claims and demands'.[22]

The London office was a vital connection for the West Country-based firm to get to the heart of its potential customers, particularly, publishers. One contract of great significance to the partnership was that for the printing of *Home Words: for Heart and Hearth*. James Nisbet & Co. and the Religious Book and Tract Society published the works 'conducted' by Rev. Charles Bullock whose volumes Butler and Tanner would eventually print, up until the Second World War when circumstances beyond their control would intervene. With closely packed lines of text, elaborate dropped capitals, a great number of illustrations and fancy borders, the pages demonstrate some of the skills employed by the compositors and printers at the firm during that period.

Butler and Tanner not only printed the *Somerset and Wilts. Journal*, they also featured within in it from time to time. In one such instance a meeting of the Local Board, held in September 1872, discussed an application from three local businesses, Butler and Tanner included,

Page from Home Words for Heart and Hearth (1873) depicting the complexity and quality of the typesetting and printing

for the use of steam whistles to indicate the beginning and end of the working day. Much debate ensued on this measure which it was claimed would 'threaten the peace and quiet of the town.' Similarly, the journal was employed in the advertising of vacancies within the firm. One such advertisement, again in 1872, aimed at the town's parents asked, 'To

Parents, Messrs Butler and Tanner have vacancies for two or three intelligent, well educated lads as apprentices in their Machine and Book-Binding Departments. Wanted also, half a dozen boys over 13 years of age.'[23]

The Sunday School infant classroom at the Zion Congregational Church

Not only was Joseph Tanner thus far a successful businessman and fair employer, his philanthropic endeavours had also benefitted the town. For example, in one act of particular generosity he had contributed to the education of its youngsters. One of his acquaintances from the Zion Chapel describes the project funded by his colleague, thus:

In March 1875 Mr Joseph Tanner announced his willingness to erect a new infant classroom at his own expenses so it was resolved to pull down the old room, level the ground and make a new approach from Whittox Lane at a cost of £65.12s.[24]

In fact, aside from running his business, Joseph Tanner was also a 'leading spirit in the Council... ....and an active supporter of his own political party'.[25] With Butler increasingly distancing himself from the partnership, it was to be Joseph Tanner who would take the business forward.

Endnotes

[1] John Rhode, *A Hundred Years of Printing: 1795–1895,* Butler and Tanner Ltd, Frome and London, 1927, p. 24.

[2] Information based on research document by Margery Hyde (D8378), Frome Museum, Frome, Somerset.

[3] *Ibid.*

[4] John Rhode, *A Hundred Years of Printing: 1795–1895,* Butler and Tanner Ltd, Frome and London, 1927, p. 30.

[5] *Ibid.,* p. 34.

[6] *Ibid.,* p. 81.

[7] *Ibid.,* p. 35.

[8] Derek Gill, *Bath Street, Frome,* Derek Gill, Frome, 1992, pp. 70–71.

[9] *Langford's Frome Almanack and West of England Advertiser*, 1854, Butler and Tanner Archive (D5405), Frome Museum, Frome, Somerset.

[10] John Rhode, *A Hundred Years of Printing: 1795–1895,* Butler and Tanner Ltd, Frome and London, 1927, pp. 44–46.

[11] 'Articles of Partnership, Mr W.T. Butler and Mr Joseph Tanner', 2nd September, 1863. Butler and Tanner Archive (DB4779/D7713/1), Frome Museum, Frome, Somerset.

[12] John Rhode, *A Hundred Years of Printing: 1795–1895,* Butler and Tanner Ltd, Frome and London, 1927, p. 54.

[13] Birth certificate of Joseph Tanner, Butler and Tanner Archive (DB4774/D7829), Frome, Somerset.

[14] Flyer: The Selwood Printing Works, Frome, Sixth Annual Wayzgoose', 10th July, 1869. Butler and Tanner Archive (DB2863/D1582), Frome Museum, Frome, Somerset.

[15] Deeds and Conveyance documentation, Butler and Tanner Archive (DB3098/D1801), Frome Museum, Frome, Somerset.

[16] 'Memorandum of Temporary Arrangement between Mr W.T. Butler and Mr Joseph Tanner, Junior.' 2nd September, 1863. Butler and Tanner Archive (DB4779/DD7712), Frome Museum, Frome, Somerset.

[17] 'Letter of Agreement, W.T. Butler and J. Tanner, 30th January, 1864. Butler and Tanner Archive (DB4779/D7717), Frome Museum, Frome, Somerset.

[18] John Rhode, *A Hundred Years of Printing: 1795–1895,* Butler and Tanner Ltd, Frome and London, 1927, p. 63.

[19] Cuzner's Hand Book to Froome Selwood, *c.* 1868, S. Cuzner, Froome-Selwood, c. 1868, pp. 134–5.

[20] 'Agreement between Mr William Thomas Butler and Mr Joseph Tanner on Dissolution of Partnership', 9th September, 1868. Butler and Tanner Archive (DB4779/D7712), Frome Museum, Frome, Somerset.

[21] 'Deed of Release and New Arrangement as within Partnership to be dissolved', 10th December, 1873, Butler and Tanner Archive (DB4779/D7714), Frome Museum, Frome, Somerset.

[22] Letter under seal, 15th January, 1879, Butler and Tanner Archive (DB4774/D7771/38), Frome Museum, Frome, Somerset.

[23] *The Newsletter: Journal of the House of Butler & Tanner Ltd.*, No. 97 September–October 1966, Butler and Tanner, Frome, p. 10.

[24] W.J. Harvey, *The Story of Zion Congregational Church, Frome,* Harvey & Woodland Ltd., 1918, p. 12. pp. 134–5

[25] John Rhode, *A Hundred Years of Printing: 1795–1895,* Butler and Tanner Ltd, Frome and London, 1927, p. 56.

Sole Proprietor: Joseph Tanner

Joseph Tanner

Throughout the nineteenth century there was exceptional growth in the printing trade. With increased mechanisation encompassing the whole of the printing and book manufacturing business the resultant lower production costs, together with mass literacy, ensured an ever-growing market. For those willing to invest in the technology and with good business acumen it was the perfect time to build a successful printing business. Joseph Tanner was one such man and during his partnership with Butler he had been responsible for driving the business's momentum. This he achieved by embracing technology and expanding the premises as, and when, necessary to accommodate the huge machinery required for the printing and production of books.

A recurrent theme throughout the history of the firm (and undoubtedly in all other mechanised industries) was that of man versus machine. When deciding whether to invest in the technology, a calculation would have been made to determine the cost of purchasing the expensive equipment against the expenditure saved in 'man hours', thus wages. The firm had steadily increased its plant from nine machines and four working presses in 1868, adding three more machines in 1872. In 1868 the working week comprised 58.5 hours which, by 1872, had decreased to 54.5 hours; reducing to 54 in 1892.[1] The parting between Butler and Tanner was finalised in January of 1879 by a letter under seal which 'mutually terminated and put an end to arrangements between them re: Printing Business in Frome and London known as Butler and Tanner'.[2] As sole proprietor he was free to continue as he had during the final years of the partnership when he had been running the Frome print works so, whilst in essence nothing had really changed he may have felt the extra weight of his sole responsibility for such a large workforce.

Aside from running a complex and demanding business, Joseph had to deal with some difficult family matters around this time. His father, Joseph, had died the previous year (1878)[3] and his ailing mother, Maria[4], was to join him in the family grave the following year (1880). Joseph had dealt with funeral arrangements for both parents and made provision for his mother's details to be added to his father's gravestone.[5] The family's plot resides in the town's Dissenters' Cemetery. The following year he was dealing with the sale of a property (Welford Villa) in which, under the terms of the grandfather's will, he, his siblings and cousin were each to receive a share. The cousin, William Fernie was working in the engineer's office of the Chicago and North Western Railway Company at the time so all the necessary transactions were being undertaken on his behalf by Joseph. Letters confirmed the sale and Joseph duly wired the money £154.17*s*.0*d*. to William, once the sale had been concluded, by the end of 1881.[6] He was also left dividends in the firm by his grandfather. Joseph paid close regard to his religious duties and remained an active member of the Zion Congregational Church. As its Chairman and a pillar of society, one of his duties was to teach in its Sunday school. One particular student, a teenage Fred Knee recalls, rather disrespectfully, one such lesson:

> Sunday 23 August, 1885
>
> 'Went to Sunday School, where Mr Tanner taught us. He has been to the Lake District,
>
> and, as usual, finished up with some nonsense...'[7]

Joseph certainly did not neglect his business whilst dealing with these family issues and civic duties. It continued to thrive and was fast becoming a major employer in the town. From such humble beginnings had grown a truly impressive printing establishment employing a multitude of tradesmen: engineers, millwrights, smiths, carpenters, roller-casting hands and knife grinders, to name but a few. The works would have been full of hustle and bustle

The Selwood Printing Works

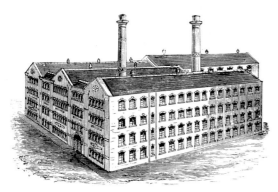

The Selwood Printing Works c. 1885

with a six-day working week comprising long working days. The physical growth of the accommodation can be clearly seen when comparing the illustration from 1860 [see chapter one] to those from 1875 and a decade later in 1885.

Joseph continued to expand the firm, purchasing new machinery and enlarging the factory to accommodate the ever increasing demand for their services. By 1895 the factory was an impressive building rising four storeys high but with the addition of two basement levels totalled six floors. Two steam beam engines powered a total of 38 printing machines which coped with a capacity of 13.5 million sheets each year. The top floors were used for the composition of journals whereas the second floor housed the book setting department and was also used for the storage of type. The ground and first floors accommodated the machine rooms and the two underground floors comprised fireproof stores.[8] The ground floor contained the largest of the machine rooms known as the 'colour room' where presses could undertake colour printing (predominantly for book covers).[9] Several hundred employees worked a fifty hour week. Years earlier, Joseph had given much thought to ways in which these employees could be given a sense of belonging to the firm and encouraged them to take responsibility for their actions within the workplace. In a letter to staff written at Christmas 1889 he shared his ideas for a future profit-sharing scheme with them. Addressing them as 'My dear friends and fellow workers', he wrote:

…The question of relations of capital and labour – how to manifestly harmonise their interest – is one that has occupied my thoughts, more or less since 1863, when I joined Mr Butler in the development of this business and during the twenty-one years I have carried it alone…

…My plan is to simply to continue to make a yearly valuation of profits in exactly the same way, and on the same principles that I have done ever since I have been in business, and for the profits to be so calculated and arrived at, to allot a certain definite proportion to be divided to every worker, according to the amounts of the total earnings of each during the previous twelve months...

...I would ask of you all to consider carefully the question of the large amounts of leakage of profit which is constantly occurring, leakage which if reduced in the future would add to the amount available for division amongst yourselves: windows broken; time lost at stopping and starting again at work; work spoiled through want of legitimate care; type in pye just thrown on one side or into display cases; matter when broken not cleared away, types dropped and trodden on rather than picked up; waste of material generally; a spirit of satisfaction with slow, lifeless, and inefficient work; gas allowed to flare away unchecked, though no longer needed and various other ways you know more about than I do...

It wasn't just the problem of wastage that had given Joseph cause for concern; amongst other worries was the continual threat of a potential fire in such an environment. Insurance against fire was a necessity and it was vital that all employees played their part in preventing the causes of any combustion. Posters were displayed around the works in order to remind workers of the rules:

To be strictly observed:
1 If any paper be hung to dry, see that the lines are quite clear of any artificial light.
2 Candles must not be used.
3 Lighting up to be done only by authorised persons. NEVER USE PAPER TORCHES.
4 Not more than a quart of Benzine, Turpentine or other spirit should be deposited in the building, and it must always be kept a safe distance from any artificial light.
5 ALL WORKROOMS MUST BE SWEPT OUT BEFORE LOCKING UP, and the sweepings removed out of the building.
6 Concealed spaces and corners must be kept clean.
7 No smoking allowed anywhere on the premises.
8 See that appliances for extinguishing fire are kept in good order.[10]

During this period the printing would have been carried out on letterpress machinery. This oldest and most simple method of printing involves the application of ink to a raised surface, reversed words or images, which are then inked and pressed onto the paper to give a positive representation. Letterpress printing can be implemented by way of either a flat-bed machine which, as the name implies, utilises a 'forme or other horizontal mounting of type and blocks', or by a rotary press which has a printing surface that is a 'wrap-round plate fitted to a rotary cylinder.'[11] Presses owned by Butler and Tanner by

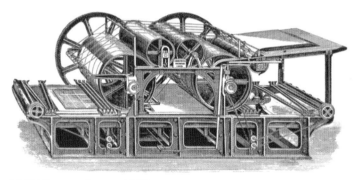

A Middleton perfector c. 1895

the end of the nineteenth century included the Middleton perfectors. Young lads were employed as 'fly boys' whose occupation involved lying on the board below the cylinders to pull the sheets of paper down.[12]

In March 1895 Joseph's thoughts turned to retirement and he passed the business to his sons, Russell and Lanfear. The value of the outstanding book debts was agreed at £19,783.12*s*.3*d*. this sum to be paid to Joseph and it was also agreed that if any monies owed to them gained interest or the sum paid to them was more than the agreed figure the difference would be paid to Joseph or his estate. [13] Remaining a family firm, Butler and Tanner was to be run jointly by the brothers, both of whom would 'become and remain partners of the firm Selwood Printing Works'.[14] An announcement in the London Gazette made the transfer publicly known:

> NOTICE is hereby given that the business of Printing and kindred trades which has for some time past been carried on by the undersigned Joseph Tanner under the style of Butler and Tanner at the Selwood Printing Works Frome in the county of Somerset has as from the 31st day of March last been this day transferred to the undersigned Russell Robson Tanner M.A. (Cambridge) and Lanfear Robson Tanner M.A. (Cambridge) who have been associated with the said Joseph Tanner in its conduct during the past ten years and that all the debts due to or owing by the old firm will be received and paid by the said Russell Robson Tanner and Lanfear Robson Tanner by whom the said business will as from that day be carried on under the old name of Butler and Tanner.
> Dated this 22nd day of May 1895.
> JOSEPH TANNER.
> RUSSELL R. TANNER.
> LANFEAR R. TANNER.[15]

For the workers, traditions continued with that year's annual works' outings still being arranged in the usual manner but it was certainly an end of an era. A trip to Stourton was undertaken for the compositors' wayzgoose, in July 1896.

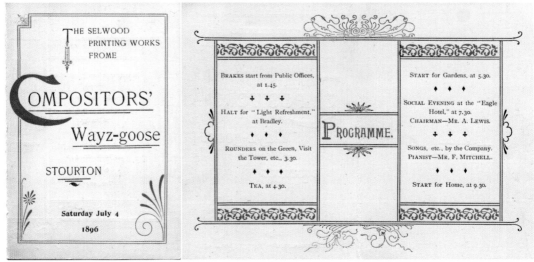

Printed programme for the compositors' 1896 annual wayzgoose [note the attractive layout displaying their composing skills]

During his years at the helm, Joseph had built up a fine business printing books for such publishers as Chatto & Windus Ltd, Ward Lock & Co. Ltd, George Bell, F. Warne & Co. Ltd, Sonnenschein & Co, Hodder & Stoughton Ltd , the Sunday School Union, the British

Colophons used by Butler and Tanner

Gospel Book Association, the Salvation Army and Dr Barnardo. Joseph Tanner's influence and business expertise should not be underestimated for, whilst it cannot be argued that the firm foundation was steadily built up by Langford and Butler, the rate of progress and growth on Joseph's watch had been remarkable.

His business acumen has been well illustrated but he was also described as 'a very humane employer' and it was his 'boast that he knew every employee personally, and if any were in trouble he did what he could to lighten the burden.' He was a regular visitor to the British School and was 'its most liberal financial supporter'. [15] Sadly, Joseph didn't have the opportunity to enjoy a long retirement, for in April 1896, he died, aged sixty. However, his great achievement remained a legacy for his descendants spanning more than a century following his death. He was laid to rest with his parents in the Dissenters' Cemetery in

Frome. The firm's future lay in the hands of two of his sons who would be charged with guiding the business into the twentieth century.

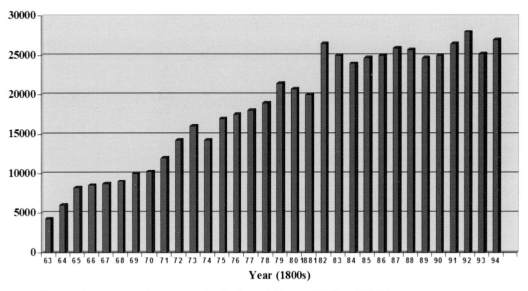

Reams of paper printed per annum by Butler and Tanner 1863 to 1894[16]

In loving memory of Joseph Tanner of Frome, died 18 February 1878 aged 79

Maria Tanner his wife, died 1 October 1880 aged 73

Joseph Tanner of Frome & Clifton died 23 April 1896 aged 60

Fanny Tanner his wife died 12 December 1904 aged 68

Margaret Robson Perowne daughter of Joseph & Fanny Tanner died 9 April 1944 aged 77

The Tanner family gravestone situated in the Dissenters' Cemetery, Frome

Endnotes

[1] John Rhode, *A Hundred Years of Printing: 1795–1895,* Butler and Tanner Ltd, Frome and London, 1927, pp. 66–68.

[2] 'Letter under Seal, W.T. Butler and Joseph Tanner, 15th January, 1879. Butler and Tanner Archive (DB4774/D7771/38), Frome Museum, Frome, Somerset.

[3] Undertakers' receipt for the estate of the late Joseph Tanner, 4th September, 1878. Butler and Tanner Archive (DB4774/D7771/37), Frome Museum, Frome, Somerset.

[4] Doctor's invoices for attendance to Mrs Tanner for years 1878 and 1879. Butler and Tanner Archive (DB4774/D7771/37), Frome Museum, Frome, Somerset.

[5] Undertakers' receipt for the Executors of the late Mrs Tanner, Christmas 1880. Butler and Tanner Archive (DB4774/D7771/37), Frome Museum, Frome, Somerset.

[6] Letters from William Fernie, Engineer's Office, Chicago and North Western Railway Co., 20th May, 1881 and 24th August, 1881. Butler and Tanner Archive (DB4774/D7771/38), Frome Museum, Frome, Somerset.

[7] David Englander, *The Diary of Fred Knee*, Society for the Study of Labour History, 1977.

[8] Joseph Tanner, 'A Selwood Scrapbook', p. 14 [unpublished notes], Butler and Tanner Archive (DB5884/L2692), Frome, Somerset.

[9] *Ibid.*

[10] 'The Selwood Printing Works, Frome, Regulations in Connection with Fire Insurance', 1887. Butler and Tanner Archive (DB3623/D3455), Frome Museum, Frome. Somerset.

[11] David Carey, *'How it Works': Printing Processes* (Loughborough: Ladybird Books Ltd: 1971), p. 34.

[12] Joseph Tanner, 'A Selwood Scrapbook', p. 16 [unpublished notes], Butler and Tanner Archive (DB5884/L2692), Frome, Somerset.

[13] 'Agreement between Joseph Tanner Esq. and Messrs. Russell Robson Tanner and Lanfear Robson Tanner as to Book Debts', 13th March, 1895. Butler and Tanner Archive (DB4779/D7715/2), Frome Museum, Frome. Somerset.

[14] 'Messrs. Butler and Tanner Articles of Partnership', 30th March, 1895. Butler and Tanner Archive (DB4779/D7713/4), Frome Museum, Frome, Somerset.

[15] *The London Gazette,* 28th May, 1895.

[16] Data from chart in John Rhode, *A Hundred Years of Printing:* 1795-1895 Butler and Tanner Ltd, Frome and London, 1927.

THREE

Into the Twentieth Century

The brothers' period of proprietorship was gravely affected by the First World War which would influence trading conditions and cause many difficulties for all British industry, including the printing trade. Disruption to the supply of paper and other raw materials required for printing and the subsequent rises in the price of paper would affect both printers and publishers. Additionally, distribution was adversely affected by the restrictive wartime conditions, whilst workers would be lost (some permanently) in the population's patriotic response to serve their country when threatened.

Joseph Tanner ensured his sons the benefit of a good education with only his youngest boys finally taking over the business. Born in 1864, Russell Robson Tanner was educated at Mill Hill School in London before studying for his Bachelor of Arts degree at Cambridge University from 1882 until 1885, subsequently acquiring his Master of Arts degree in 1889.[1] In his youth he was a member of Clifton Rugby Football Club (1884 to 1885), and, as an adult, served as Justice of the Peace for Somerset from 1896[2]. He was promoted from the rank of Captain to Major in the 3rd Volunteer Battalion, Prince Albert's (Somerset Light Infantry) toward the end of 1914.[3] He married Florence Evans in 1889.[4] Lanfear Robson Tanner, born in 1865 was also educated at Mill Hill in London. He followed in his brother's footsteps, entering Cambridge University in 1883 to study for his Bachelor of Arts degree obtained in 1886, followed by a Master of Arts degree in 1891. He married Nellie Trotman in 1897 and served as Justice of the Peace for Somerset in 1917.[5]

Joseph had two elder sons, neither of whom joined Russell and Lanfear in the business. His eldest son, Joseph Robson Tanner, was born in Frome in 1860 and also educated at Mill Hill School before entering St. John's College at Cambridge University in 1879. Obtaining a Bachelor of Arts degree in 1883 and a Master of Arts degree in 1886, he never participated in his father's business preferring the life of an academic and remained with the university for his entire career. He gained his doctorate in 1905, having married Charlotte Larkman in 1888 and taught Indian history between 1885 and 1893, served as a tutor from 1900 to 1912 and tutorial bursar (1900 to 1921), becoming a fellow of the college from 1886 until his death in 1931.[6] As a historian he wrote and edited several volumes, primarily those related to Samuel Pepys.[7]

Joseph's second eldest son, Edgar Robson Tanner, also chose not to enter the family firm preferring to practise law instead. He gained a Bachelor of Arts degree in 1884 and a Master of Arts degree in 1888. He worked as a solicitor from 1900 to 1946 in both Bristol and London, marrying Marion Button in 1888.[8]

With Russell and Lanfear at the helm following the retirement and death of their father the enterprise was prepared for the new century. Having grown so rapidly and successfully under Joseph's control the most pressing problem facing the brothers was a lack of space. Their existing site, situated so closely within the confines of the town could not be expanded any further so it was decided to look out of the Trinity area for any suitable building land. When searching it would have seemed an eminently sensible idea to consider methods of transportation, in particular the town's connections to the rest of the country by means of the Great Western Railway.

By the turn of the century the business had grown with many of the townspeople employed in the various departments of the Selwood premises. The camaraderie between working colleagues extended into various leisure activities and works' outings included those undertaken by individual departments. A 1900 day trip (no longer referred to as the wayzgoose) for the compositors, involved a journey to nearby Shearwater (via Longleat) and Warminster, the cost of which was 3*s*.6*d*. for each member to contribute. The itinerary gives a charming reminder of what could be expected and what was expected of them.

It was Russell Tanner who was to introduce 'monotype' to the firm. In 1898, the establishment was an 'open house' with around 25 members of the Typographical Association and when, in 1900, the business was approached by the association with a request to increase wages to 26*s*. per week, the response was that in order to earn that sum they would have to increase their productivity from 49,000 'ens'[9] a week to 53,000 and those who could not would be dismissed. Following a twelve month trial, only ten of the fifty had been able to work at the required pace. When the association requested that the

A beautifully crafted card for the compositors' 1900 outing

wage increase remain but the rate to be reduced, the proprietors declined. As a result the association declared the print works 'an unrecognised office' and its members either departed or were expelled by their union. With the firm recruiting compositors from elsewhere, serious riots broke out as they were prevented from entering the factory.[10] In 1901 they installed monotype keyboards and casters and by 1903 there were six casters with nineteen keyboards (fifteen of which were operated by female employees).[11] Representatives of the firm may well have visited the Frome Electricity Exhibition held in 1903 for, in 1904, they replaced the steam as power source for the presses with electricity. An agreement was set up between them and Messrs Edmundson's Electricity Corporation Ltd to supply all power and electricity at Selwood Printing Works.[12] Steam power was, however, being utilised by Russell Tanner in his chosen mode of transportation. He owned an American steam-powered car which 'put out super-heated steam at knee height on the pavement side'[13], no doubt putting fear into any of Frome's pedestrians he encountered.

Records show that between the years of 1907 and 1922 the firm's income from printing was further supplemented by dividends, rental income and loan interest from such sources as: Adderwell Allotments (Rent); Bank Interest; Culliford, City of Saratoft, Russia (Rent); Electricity Supply (Rent of Radley Villa); Frome Fanciers Association (Loan); Great Western Railway (Dividends); Lanston Monotype Corporation (Dividends); National Telephone Co.; 50, Orchard Street (Rent); Randall and Sons (Dividends); Dr Seddon

(Rent); Spiers and Pond (Dividends); Victoria Hospital (Dividends); Whiting (Rent); War Bonds (Dividends) and Warne & Co. Ltd (Dividends).[14] This list is fascinating in that it indicates the diversity of the proprietors' interests geographically; they supported local institutions such as Frome's Victoria Hospital as well as having property interests in Russia; but also in technological terms with investments in the Great Western Railway and Lanston Monotype Corporation; as well as in political terms with its national interests in War Bonds.

The rural plot before being built upon by Butler and Tanner

By 1907 Russell and Lanfear had found a suitable parcel of land, conveniently placed by the town's railway station. Over the next two years they purchased eight acres of land in the Adderwell area of Frome, the first from a retired builder: George Coleman Williams on 20th July, 1907[15]. Other parcels of land were purchased in the vicinity during 1907 and 1908 including some from the Marquis of Bath.[16] The land was far from easy to turn into a suitable building plot, however, for it sloped steeply toward the river. Over two hundred men were employed simply to level the site prior to building.[17]

Whilst all this expansion was being undertaken the presses continued to run and the firm's income remained steady. The plant being used in the 'Furnival' room by 1907 included two web-fed rotaries, a two-colour Koenig & Bauer cylinder press and the two-colour press manufactured by the American Kidder Press Company. These were used for printing the monthly magazine *Home Words* the print runs of which topped 800,000 copies.[18] The majority of the book printing was carried out on presses using stereotyped plates well into the twentieth century. Rotary plates were cast flat then bent

The Kidder Rotary Press as seen in the bottom corner of a ticket for the 1880 'Printing, Stationery and Kindred Trades Exhibition and Market'

around the plate cylinders whilst the metal was still hot. A very skilled craft, the job of the stereotyper involved the making and correcting of plates, the mounting of blocks and the manufacturing of accented letters, when necessary.[19]

In 1910, carrying on their father's practice of investment in new technology, the brothers purchased a huge reel-fed perfecting rotary press from the German company Koenig & Bauer. Known affectionately as the 'Dreadnought' because of its enormous size, the press had great capacity. It printed up to 224 pages per revolution and prevented paper creasing or cracking by using a steam chest to regulate the paper's humidity.[20] This mighty machine was to provide many years of service, running 'virtually day and night until 1972'.[21] The 'Dreadnought' joined the two other rotary presses: one known as the 'Variable' installed in 1908 which was an extra quad-demy all-size and another,

The 'Dreadnought' in action during the 1950s. The proximity of the employees indicates the sheer scale of the machine

unsurprisingly, known as the 'Fixed' installed in 1909 which was a quad-demy fixed-size printing press.[22]

With the business continually growing larger and by now split over two sites it was inevitable that work's outings for all employees were no longer possible but socialising within Butler and Tanner did continue. For over the next century Butler and Tanner could be counted amongst the most sociable enterprises in the town. Separate departmental events were eventually supplemented with an organised social committee and purpose-built premises for the explicit purpose of staff getting together outside working hours. In these early days, however, the more formal departmental events continued. One example, the composing department dinner and concert held 4th January, 1910 at The Swan, Badcox included dinner, songs and toasts, indicated that Butler and Tanner workers certainly knew how to entertain themselves.[23] Another department, possibly the bindery, can be seen pictured in anticipation of their own excursion.[24]

A particularly elaborately crafted card for the compositors' dinner in 1910, demonstrating the pride in their workmanship

A departmental outing in 1910

In 1911, a legal document was drawn up to include supplemental articles of partnership implementing changes to a clause which would give power to the other partner in the event of 'death, bankruptcy or lunacy' of the other.[25]

Plant during this period included four platens, four small Wharfedales and three big two-colour Wharfedales, all of which would have been hand fed. The two-colour Wharfedales were huge and developed from stop cylinder machines. According to Joe Tanner (junior), their disadvantages lay in the fact that with the cylinder having to revolve twice having taken the sheet of paper to allow the two formes to pass underneath, then stop to allow the formes to return to their original position, output remained slow. Additionally, because 'both formes used a common impression cylinder, local adjustment to pressure on the cylinder itself was not possible where the colours overlapped.'[26] By 1911 the Kidder two-colour rotary press had been fitted with a Koenig and Bauer folder and moved to the Adderwell premises. This was joined by the two-colour six-cylinder Koenig & Bauer press and a new reel-fed four-colour letterpress rotary. The last of the Middleton Perfectors had been scrapped by 1911. Unafraid of experimentation, Russell Tanner first tried the process of photogravure for the illustrations of the *Home Words* journal, in 1912. However, the machinery was soon

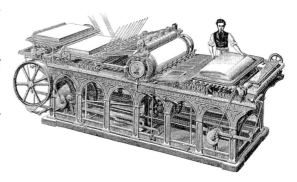

A Brehmer press, similar to the Wharfedales in use at Butler and Tanner

A Koenig and Bauer four-colour web press

sold as it proved unsuccessful: the long run of paper needed to allow the gravure illustrations to dry before the text could be printed on it (over 300 feet) made it impossible to hold register.[27]

Learning the printing trade was a long and difficult affair from which true tradesmen emerged. The quality of workmanship within the print works was extremely high and anyone who didn't pass muster was dismissed. Apprenticeships lasted for seven years and the majority stayed in the print works to serve the Company well for many years. The illustration of the indenture certificate for one such apprentice, Harry Hall, from 1913, gives an indication of the wages paid and the terms and conditions of his apprenticeship.

The First World War (1914 to 1918) affected the business of Butler and Tanner with many workers joining up to serve their country. This is shown in the employees' records which indicate those workers who joined up to serve their country in H.M. Forces or for associated war work. Their fates are known, for their employee records were subsequently updated when they returned to work or, sadly, for others who died during the war. Other than the employee records there is little company documentation for the period so it is difficult to say just how much the business was affected. However, it is known that generally throughout the period there was a scarcity of paper and raw materials causing production difficulties with a resultant fall in the number of new book titles from 12,379 in 1913 to 7,716 in 1918[28] and this must have impacted upon Butler and Tanner.

Those employees who returned after the war had 'gone as apprentices and youths, but had returned men'[29]. This gave them the confidence to stand up for the rights of workers in a way that may have seemed unthinkable before the War. With increasing interest in the Trade Union movement from the returning men, they approached the proprietors about

Illustration of framed Apprenticeship Indenture Certificate

the possibility of making the printers a Trade Union shop. Met with obvious initial reluctance, negotiations resulted in the firm being described as a '100 per cent TU office in March 1920.'[30]

The Tanner family had been personally affected by the First World War: Russell's son, Gerald Russell Tanner was killed. At the age of twenty he had joined up in 1914. Having seen much service and being injured on three separate occasions, he died of his wounds in 1918.[31] He was awarded the Military Cross. Russell's other son, Humphrey, fought with the 1st/4th Battalion Somerset Light Infantry and was wounded in the leg.[32] As the family were financially secure and enjoyed a high standard of living, they participated in local philanthropic and charitable activities. Unfortunately, on one occasion they found themselves victims of crime: Lanfear and Ellen Tanner's house was broken into over the

Donald Vaughan Tanner

Whitsun holiday of 1920 whilst they were away. They must have been shocked and saddened upon their return to discover that jewellery and cash (collected for charity) had been stolen.[33]

On 30th April, 1921 Lanfear Robson Tanner died and in his will, written only days earlier, he had bequeathed his business interest to his son, Donald Vaughan Tanner.[34] With both branches of the family owning the business discussions must have taken place with a view to securing its future. The following year, a formal valuation was undertaken specifying a total value of £102,960.15s.3d. for the freehold land and buildings: steam; heating; gas and water services, steam and electric motive power and electric light installation; plant and machinery; trade fixtures; loose tools; utensils and belting; office furniture and fittings and motor vehicles.

Decisions were made between the two families and following the valuation the partnership changed its status to that of a limited company in 1923: the terms thus demonstrated:

Memorandum and Articles of Association of Butler and Tanner Limited

Incorporated 23rd July 1923

3(b) To carry on all or any of the business of printers, lithographers, type-founders, typesetters, stereotypers, electrotypers, photographic printers, photo-lithographers, engravers, die-sinkers, stationers, bookbinders, designers, draughtsmen, manufacturers and distributors of and dealers in paper and ink and written, engraved, painted or printed productions of all descriptions, booksellers, publishers, advertising and news agents, and dealers in or manufacturers of any articles or things of a character similar or analogous to the foregoing or any of them or connected therewith.

(c) To carry on business as proprietors, publishers, and sellers of newspapers, journals, magazines, books and other literary works and undertakings.

5 The Share Capital of the Company is £80,000 divided into 80,000 shares of £1 each.

Russell R. Tanner, Lansdown Grove Lodge, Bath

Printer

One Share

Humphrey V. Tanner, Lansdown Grove Lodge, Bath

Printer

One Share

30,000 Preference Shares (these had the right to 6% cumulative preferential dividend)

50,000 Ordinary Shares

Date of document 18th July 1923

Lanfear's widow, Ellen Tanner, and Russell Tanner became principal shareholders. Russell was appointed Chairman, whilst Humphrey Russell Tanner and cousin Donald Vaughan Tanner became joint Managing Directors. The first year of trading as a limited company produced the following balance sheet: Reserves £1,000, Investments £15,317, Plant and Buildings £45,733, Undividend Profit £8,488.[35] The print works continued in much the same fashion with workers enjoying their outings within their departments.

In 1927, a terrible accident at the printing works resulted in the fatality of one of the machine feeders. In the early morning of 8th February, 37-year-old Frederick Bishop received appalling injuries from which he later died.

According to witness statements the prefactor printing machine had trouble with one of the pages and had to stop at 6.15am. At 6.30am Frederick Bishop had gone to oil the machine as was his usual duty. The trouble was explained to him and the reason for the machine being stopped. The witness had been told to then clean the machine and believed that Frederick had walked away from the machine. It was necessary to move the machine in order to clean other parts so the witness pressed the button and it moved between one and two feet whereupon he heard a groan. He applied the brake but on inspection found Frederick 'pinched', caught by a metal bar. The first aid man was called and pulled the injured man from the machine: he was taken to hospital where he died of his injuries: broken collarbone, five fractured ribs, collapsed left lung and damaged heart

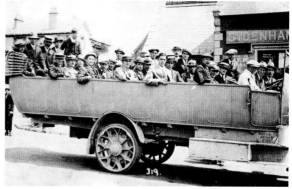

Men from the machine room before their outing to Bournemouth in 1922

Butler and Tanner bindery chapel outing c. 1926

valve. The inquest heard that the power should have been turned off but it had not been. The verdict ruled that it was an error on the part of the deceased.[36]

At a later meeting of the board of directors (held in 1929) it was confirmed that their insurance company had paid £300 compensation to Frederick Bishop's widow.

She, Lily Bishop, approached the directors in November, asking for financial assistance having spent all £300.[37] Payment of a further £100 was made following her request.[38] Frederick had first joined the Company in 1904 at the age of fourteen. He then left the firm in 1911, but had been reengaged in 1919.[39] No firm wants to deal with an industrial accident and, over the following years various safety measures were adopted. Various acts and union involvement would ultimately improve the health and safety of workers throughout the whole printing trade.

The Adderwell works continued to provide the necessary additional space and the two photographs illustrate the scale of the premises during this period. For a short time the Company was led by Humphrey and Donald Tanner as joint Managing Directors. However, it would not be long before Humphrey would become sole Managing Director. Allegedly a lover of speed, Donald had been taught to drive in the early 1920s by the firm's lorry driver, Albert Stone, and had subsequently bought a fast American car. Donald was also a keen aviator and joined the Bristol and Wessex Aeroplane Club. On 6th May, 1928 he was killed in an air crash, together with his fellow pilot Richard Hopper. The plane, a de Havilland D.H.60 Moth, spun, crashed and burned at Filton,

Exterior of the Adderwell works by the end of the 1920s

near Bristol, where the two young men lost their lives. To honour his memory, his mother, Ellen, bought the first x-ray unit for Frome Victoria Hospital.[40] Russell Robson Tanner had died in 1927 and, with the earlier loss of Lanfear, Humphrey took control of the Company. Joseph's sons had managed the firm's expansion well with the land at Adderwell becoming increasingly covered in

Interior of the Adderwell works by the end of the 1920s

works' buildings. Humphrey Tanner, aged thirty six by this stage, took charge as Chairman and Managing Director, and was to prove himself a great asset throughout the difficult decades ahead. Humphrey's son, Joseph Russell Tanner was born in 1928 and would, many years later take over the role of leading the Company in the same way his father, grandfather and namesake, great-grandfather had before him. For now, though the task was to fall upon Humphrey's shoulders.

Endnotes

[1] Cambridge, University Of. (2013). pp. 110–1. *Alumni Cantabrigienses* (Vol. 2). London: Forgotten Books. (Original work published 1922).

[2] *Kelly's Handbook to the Titled, Landed and Official Classes, 1909*, p. 1580.

[3] Supplement to the *London Gazette*, 14th November, 1914.

[4] University of Cambridge Alumni Cantabrigienses; a Biographical List of All Known Students, Graduates and Holders of Office, p. 110.

[5] *Ibid.*

[6] *Ibid.*, p. 109.

[7] *Oxford Dictionary of National Biography.*

[8] *Ibid.*

[9] An en is a typographic unit, traditionally the size of which is, the width of an uppercase letter 'N'.

[10] Joseph Tanner, 'A Selwood Scrapbook', p. 21 [unpublished notes], Butler and Tanner Archive (DB5884/L2692), Frome, Somerset.

[11] *Ibid.*, p. 22.

[12] Agreement between Messrs. Edmundson's Electricity Corporation Ltd and R.R. Tanner and L.R. Tanner Esqs., 18th August, 1904. Butler and Tanner Archive (DB4779/D7794), Frome Museum, Frome, Somerset.

[13] Joseph Tanner, 'A Selwood Scrapbook', p. 18 [unpublished notes], Butler and Tanner Archive (DB5884/L2692), Frome, Somerset.

[14] 'Receivable: Interest, Rent; Sundries 1907 to 1922', Butler and Tanner Archive, Frome Museum, Frome, Somerset.

15 Deed for land at Adderwell between George Coleman Williams, Retired Builder, and Russell Robson Tanner and Lanfear Robson Tanner, 20th July, 1907. Butler and Tanner Archive (DB3098/D1801), Frome Museum, Frome, Somerset.

16 Deed for land at Adderwell between Marquis of Bath and Rev. Can. Hon. Sidney Meade and Russell Robson Tanner, 25th March, 1908. Butler and Tanner Archive (DB3098/D1801), Frome Museum, Frome, Somerset.

17 *The Butler and Tanner Group Newsletter*, Issue No. 3, October 1994, p. 13.

18 *The Butler and Tanner Group Newsletter*, Issue No. 19, February 2000, pp. 46–47.

19 Joseph Tanner, 'A Selwood Scrapbook', p. 25 [unpublished notes], Butler and Tanner Archive (DB5884/L2692), Frome, Somerset.

20 'A short history of Butler and Tanner', article in Butler and Tanner Archive (D8652 and DB5706), Frome Museum, Frome. Somerset.

21 Harry Bellows, *The Newsletter: Journal of the House of Butler and Tanner Ltd*, August 1991, No. 6, p. 30.

22 *Ibid.*

23 Programme: Composing Dept. Dinner and Concert, 4th January, 1910. Butler and Tanner Archive (DB4761/D7709), Frome Museum, Frome, Somerset.

24 *The Butler and Tanner Group Newsletter*, Issue No. 2, June 1994, p. 10.

25 'Messrs. Butler and Tanner Supplemental Articles of Partnership', 29th April, 1911, Butler and Tanner Archive, Frome Museum, Frome, Somerset.

26 *The Butler and Tanner Group Newsletter*, Issue No. 19, February 2000, p. 46.

27 Joseph Tanner, 'A Selwood Scrapbook', p. 30a [unpublished notes], Butler and Tanner Archive (DB5884/L2692), Frome, Somerset.

28 Ian Norrie (ed.), *Mumby's Publishing and Bookselling in the Twentieth Century*, 6th edn., (London: Bell & Hyman), 1982), p. 20.

29 *Newsletter: Journal of the House of Butler & Tanner Ltd.*, No. 126, October 1970, Butler and Tanner, Frome, p. 1.

30 *Ibid.*, p. 4.

31 'The War Dead of Christ's College Boat Club 1914–1918'.

32 David L. Adams, *Frome's Fallen Heroes: the Great War*, 2000, p. 102–103.

33 *Wells Journal*, 4th June, 1920, Wells, Somerset.

34 Will of Lanfear Robson Tanner, 16th April, 1921. Butler and Tanner Archive (DB4779/D7721), Frome Museum, Frome, Somerset.

35 'Notes for Managing Directors Reports to Board of Directors of Butler and Tanner Ltd, The Selwood Printing Works, Frome', Butler and Tanner Archive, Frome Museum, Frome, Somerset.

36 'Inquest on Frederick Bishop, Coroner 16th February, 1927'. Butler and Tanner Archive (DB5862/D9789), Frome Museum, Frome, Somerset.

37 ''Notes for Managing Directors Reports to Board of Directors of Butler and Tanner Ltd, The Selwood Printing Works, Frome', Butler and Tanner Archive, Frome Museum, Frome, Somerset.

38 'Receipt from Lily E. Bishop, 16th November, 1929', Butler and Tanner Archive (DB4774), Frome Museum, Frome, Somerset.

39 Employee Index Cards. Butler and Tanner Archive (D7690/2571), Frome Museum, Frome, Somerset.

40 *Working Memories: Frome Workers tell their Stories,* Home in Frome in association with Millstream Books, 2012, pp. 62–63.

FOUR

Humphrey Russell Tanner

Humphrey Russell Tanner

The adoption of mechanised typesetting was to characterise the first half of the twentieth century when 'virtually all commercially produced books were set by Monotype or Linotype and printed from type or relief plates' by the 1950s.[1] Butler and Tanner, continually seeking to invest in the latest developments, held shares in the Lanston Monotype Corporation from 1920 to 1922, having initially implemented the Monotype typesetting method in 1901. The firm was amongst the first of the country's book printers to realise the further potential of Monotype machinery, sending representatives to America to investigate the possibilities of the improving technology.[2] They installed an offset litho press in 1932, in anticipation of an August-Hunter photo-composition machine (of 1922) becoming available, but the device was never commercialised.[3]

Humphrey Tanner maintained meticulous notes relating to board meetings and from these can be gained a real sense of the challenges and difficulties faced by him. One of Humphrey's first acts, as Chairman of the Board, was to arrange for the building of two cottages as a way of honouring the memory of his father, Russell, and uncle, Lanfear. At a Board meeting in the summer of 1929, a tender from Z.S. Chislitt & Sons for the building of two memorial cottages for £1,175 was duly accepted and building work began.[4] Once erected, the pair of cottages built on land at Adderwell in Frome, were made available to retired employees. Butler and Tanner offered the cottages as domiciles for which they

One of the pair of memorial cottages built on the Adderwell land at Caxton Road

would charge no rent, and on which they would also pay the rates; in addition to providing a weekly pension of 10*s*. to their inhabitants. Directors were to consider applications from any eligible candidates and chose the deserving recipients at their discretion.[5]

The land at Adderwell was utilised as an extension to the firm's main site at Selwood Road, in the town. A new warehouse had been built at Adderwell, on the town's outskirts, allowing for the transference of stock from the other site. This, in itself, did not provide enough space and following a proposal that an additional wing be built onto the Adderwell premises, a tender for the work was accepted in 1929. The approved bid, made by Messrs. Blackford and Sons was for the sum of £4,745.[6] The increasing importance of the Adderwell site can be gauged

Year	Selwood	Adderwell	Total
1921	£53,794	£23,689	£77,483
1929	£81,108	£84,984	£166,092

Valuation figures for both the Selwood and Adderwell sites

from a comparison of valuation figures between both Selwood and Adderwell over a period of just eight years.

In the same year it was reported that net profits were down. The proposed remedy was the installation of new, more economical machinery, in view of the fact that work on the rotary machines had increased by forty per cent over the previous year. A visit to Germany was planned, the purpose of which was to investigate the feasibility of either overhauling their old rotary printers or replacing them. The resultant report concluded that the two-colour rotary was beyond repair but that the other machines would be repaired by fitting new parts. Two Miehle perfectors were ordered at a cost of £6,900. It was also

The eagle counterweight from the Columbian press

decided in 1929, to increase considerably the Company's stocks of both cloth and thread, 'in view of the position in the cotton industry'.[7] In general, their printing machinery was in use for a great number of years and only scrapped when obsolete or where the cost of repair outweighed its value. One particular manufacturer of letterpress machinery produced the Columbian press, easily distinguishable by its counterweight in the form of an American eagle. Mr Butler's establishment housed two such presses and these can be seen in the illustration from 1863 in the first chapter. One such counterweight was retained by Butler and Tanner after the machinery had been scrapped, and was, in later years, affectionately known as 'Mr Joe's eagle'.[8]

At the beginning of the new decade, the additional Adderwell wing had been completed and the perfectors up and running alongside another small perfector that had also been purchased. The old Wharfedale presses had been disposed of and it was agreed that, as the old press being used to print *Home Words* was at least thirty years old by this point, a new rotary press was to be bought for the purpose. In addition, The Great Western Railway had awarded Butler and Tanner an additional five years to the contract for the printing of its *Holiday Haunts*: a fact which necessitated an investment in additional sewing machines.

In early 1931 it was concluded by the Board of Directors that the previous year

The Miehle perfector c. 1929

A copy of Holiday Haunts printed for the Great Western Railway

had been a bad year for the business and, indeed, for the book trade as a whole. After the trip to Germany to investigate offset printing it was deemed that there would be no justification for installing plant that 'at the present seems largely experimental'. They did, however, order a new rotary press from an English company (The Nathen Press Engineering Company), employed for the fulfilment of the *Home Words* contract. With investment in new machinery, the cost of wages was lowered as less manual labour was required. It was reported that the Company's wage bill had been reduced by £7,000 due to the increased expenditure on plant. In order to undertake the printing and binding of one shilling novels the demand for which had increased, it was also decided to install a new folding machine and automatic feeder at a cost of £1,500. As was common with printing establishments, more storage space was always needed. It was decided to move all the new machines into the Adderwell premises so as to use the Selwood premises for valuable warehouse storage. An additional 25ft was added to the Adderwell chimney at a cost of £170 necessary because, as Humphrey explained, 'in certain winds smuts get into the factory and spoil a certain quantity of our work.'[9]

Business failed to improve the following year. This general downturn in the book trade was signified to Butler and Tanner when publishers began to order fewer copies for each print run.

The extended chimney at the Adderwell works

However, the directors could not be accused of failing to invest and a proposal was made for the installation of a Smythe rounding and backing machine for £1,750 to replace the 18 year old R and B machines. At a meeting in June, 1932 the board was presented with a proposal to install equipment for the photo offset process in the belief that turnover would increase by £10,000 to £15,000 per annum. It was supposed that the cost would be between £2,500 and £3,500. By November of that year an order had been placed for a Mann[10] offset machine for £1,450. It was agreed that the photographic side of the process (i.e. plates) would be made in London initially until they were confident in their proficiency with the press printing side. With business suffering from the downturn in trade it was suggested that to attract more contracts it would be necessary to lower the prices of their services. The Binders Union received notice from the Master Binders Association of a fifteen per cent wage reduction. Butler and Tanner would abide by this if the Joint Industrial Council of the Trade agreed a reduction.

Notwithstanding the economic depression, staff socials continued. An employees' outing, organised for the summer of 1929, involved a fair amount of logistical planning. Departing Frome by train the group first went to Windsor to visit the castle followed by lunch and afternoon tea on saloon steamers *Viscount* and *Hampton Court*.[11] Judging by the fact that the meals were held in three separate sittings, it would appear that the event was well attended. The following summer a similar event involved a train trip to London and Brighton. A hearty breakfast (including such exotic fare as turbot meunière and finnan haddock) could be purchased aboard the train for the sum of 3*s.*6*d.*, whilst a glass of wine or spirits could be bought for a shilling or should a bottle of Worthington, Bass or Guinness be more to the taste, these could be had for 9*d.*[12] Despite the continuing economic depression, employees still enjoyed an outing by train to London during the summer of 1932. However, note the plainly printed programme which is vastly reduced in size from those of previous years: a real sign of austerity.

The general gloom surrounding the economic outlook for the country's business was cautiously lifted by the end of the following year. At the board meeting in November 1933,

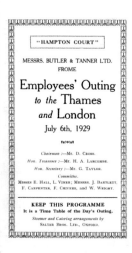

Programme for the employees' outing to London, 1929

Programme for the employees' outing to London and Brighton, 1930

the belief was stated that since August of that year there had generally been more optimism in the trade as a whole. Humphrey voiced this to his fellow directors saying, 'I think we may safely say that we have got over the centre of the depression'. The installation of a new folding machine had allowed them to 'do neat folding on machine at 10½*d*. per 1,000 sections instead of 3*s*. 5*d*. per 1,000 sections' for their production of *Holiday Haunts*.[13]

By 1934, it was generally supposed that things were looking up for their trade. Two libel actions against the firm: the publishers Thatman Butterworth Ltd being sued by Lord

Alfred Douglas and publishers Hamish Hamilton Ltd by Mr Delver had resulted in minimal costs by Butler and Tanner because

BUTLER & TANNER
LIMITED

**EMPLOYEES'
OUTING**
to
LONDON

Saturday, June 18th,
1932

TIME TABLE

FORWARD

FROME
depart - - 7 0 a.m.

WESTBURY
depart - - 7 16 a.m.

PADDINGTON
arrive - - 9 40 a.m.

RETURN

PADDINGTON
depart - - 11 50 p.m.

WESTBURY
arrive - - 1 43 a.m.

FROME
arrive - - 1 57 a.m.

Arrangements can be made for a few passengers to return at 6.0 p.m. Notification must reach Mr. G. Taylor not later than Thursday, June 16th.

Small card for the 1932 outing to London

the respective publishers had agreed to take responsibility for damages. The contract with the Great Western Railway for the printing of *Holiday Haunts* had been increased by a further six years. Permission was sought from the board to investigate abroad for colour printing due to increasing demand (especially for children's books). By the end of the year things were continuing in a more positive vein. It was recommended that repairs were necessary at the Selwood premises; additional storage was required and so the building of a new shed for such purpose was sanctioned. More Linotype composing machinery and

perfectors were installed. In the London office the gentleman in charge, Mr Aris, had 'expressed a desire to retire'. The agreed date for this was set at 30th September, 1935. Having first joined the business on 1st October, 1889, he was just one of many long-serving members of staff.

The following year, the question of printers' responsibilities in libel cases came to their attention, once again. Even though the previous two libel actions had not incurred too great a cost for Butler and Tanner, it was becoming a growing problem for the book trade.

Page from a 1934 purchase order ledger Costly libel payments were increasingly being incurred due to publishers' insurance companies who were now endeavouring to persuade the printers to accept some of the burden. Investment in plant and machinery continued apace: the Linotype composing machine, it was reported, was a great success and a proposal made to add another. They replaced the Motor Cory, and a case making machine and the purchase of a new plate shaver, at a cost of £200 was also proposed. In the foundry (at Selwood) they evolved a mounting block that enabled twenty per cent make ready time on plates. The new Adderwell warehouse had been completed and a small motor truck was purchased for the sum of £85 in order to save the cost of employing two men. A second Linotype machine was installed to work to 36 ems[14] instead of 30. However, this machine proved unsatisfactory so was returned to the manufacturer and replaced with another 30 em machine.[15]

Continued investment and improvements in efficiency helped to establish the Frome printer as one of great repute. It has been widely claimed that, in 1935 they were the chosen printer for the first ten Penguin paperbacks (published simultaneously in July by The Bodley Head, a firm founded by John Lane and Elkin Matthews in 1887): *Ariel* by André Maurois, *Farewell to Arms* by Ernest Hemingway, *Poet's Pub* by Eric Linklater, *Madame Claire* by Susan Ertz, *The Unpleasantness at the Belona Club* by Dorothy L. Sayers, *The Mysterious Affair at Styles* by Agatha Christie, *Twenty-five* by Beverley Nichols, *William* by E.H. Young, *Gone to Earth* by Mary Webb, *Carnival* by Compton Mackenzie. However, the first editions of these ten titles were actually printed by the Athenaeum Printing Works. Their claims are not without foundation though as Butler and Tanner are credited with printing the third impressions of both *Ariel* and *Madame Claire* in October 1935. In both cases the first twenty Penguin titles are printed as an advertisement on the rear cover. Ledgers reveal that they received three payments of: £319.0s.6d. and £300.0s.0d. on 4th March, 1936 and £166.19s.10d. on 2nd May, 1936 from Penguin Books Ltd. The Bodley Head had been longstanding customers of Butler and Tanner prior to this period so it is understandable that the firm would be chosen for the task. As there was such huge demand (there were three million copies printed in the first year) Penguin Books Ltd employed multiple printers including: Richard Clay & Co Ltd; Hazell, Watson & Viney Ltd; Wyman & Sons Ltd and Purnell & Sons Ltd (located in nearby Paulton) to print their books in 1935 and 1936. Humphrey had, allegedly, been sceptical about the entire project when he had first been approached by Allen Lane (John Lane's nephew who had inherited control of the firm of publishers named the Bodley Head). When asked about the possibility of printing these new paperback volumes he had replied, 'Whoever's going to buy a book bound in paper.'[16]

The following year, they joined the Master Printers Federation. Reasons given for the decision were: to ensure they had the right of appeal to the Joint Industrial Council in the event of any dispute with Unions; to ascertain agreed rates for various machines; and for free legal advice. Continually looking for ways to save money they agreed a new rate for

Examples of Butler and Tanner's colour printing of the era

electric power predicting a saving of approximately twenty five per cent (£700) over the previous rate. With the consideration of improving communication, they installed a teleprinter between Frome and the London office, initially on a three month trial. As ever, strong investment decisions continued and the purchases were made of a new wrapping machine for £900 and a colour machine at a cost of £5,000 due to increasing demand for colour work. In addition they refitted a new photographic department and experimental work at a cost of £600. In the same year they entered into a contract with the Automobile Association for three editions of the Handbook 'at an eminently satisfactory price'.[17] A group of machine minders went to the Printing Machine Exhibition on a Saturday at their own expense but were awarded five shillings from the Company. They made up the time lost in working hours the following week. Additionally, Butler and Tanner took a stand at the Sunday Times Book exhibition in 1936.

The first automatic hard-back binding line in Europe arranging free-standing 1935 American machines to feed each other; the bookbinders in charge are Fred Foster and Jack Bartlett [18]

By 1937 they had ordered yet more machinery, seen at the Printing Machine Exhibition a few months previously, comprising a Miehle two-colour press complete with self-feeder and extension for £2,800 and four new mono casters for £625 each followed a few months later by two additional mono casters at the same cost. Lack of storage facilities continued to cause acute problems and it was hoped that another building scheme for Adderwell would be able to solve this. Industrial relations were causing concern in that the New Factory Acts due to be implemented the following year could possibly adversely affect the firm, particularly rules governing girls' overtime. In addition, a reduction in working hours from 48 to 45 per week came into force in October of 1937, by agreement between the Master Printers Federation and Union. To accommodate the changes in working hours Butler and Tanner closed on a Saturday morning and worked to 6pm on Tuesdays and Thursdays instead of 5.30pm to make up the extra time. Prices were raised by five per cent to cover this. One of their regular customers, John Lane's company, the aforementioned The Bodley Head Ltd, went into liquidation in 1936. This was to cause a financial loss for Butler and Tanner as they were owed the not insignificant sum of £995 for work undertaken.[19]

In 1938, despite the threat of war (the only mention of this at the Board meeting was that an 'Air Raid Precautions Officer was to visit all factories in the district') investment in the business continued apace. A new Cundall Folder was bought to replace the twenty year

old Chambers Folder that had been causing trouble. A contract to print the Automobile Association's Handbook for a further period of five years was awarded to Butler and Tanner, 'but at a rather lower price than previously'.[20] Having placed the contract it was decided that the books were to be rounded and backed which necessitated the purchase of a new rounder and backer costing £2,000. However, to account for

Operator inputting data into the Monotype caster c. 1950

this Butler and Tanner charged £2 per 1,000 extra for doing this where the usual price was £1. To the Board's relief the lifts at the Selwood premises were passed by the Factory Inspector with very minor alterations. Humphrey Tanner reported that they had been fortunate as, had the inspector insisted 'on us conforming with the New Factory Act in its entirety, it would have been about £2,000'.[21]

Stereotyping c. 1950

It was reported that Publisher's Association sales were down twenty five per cent over the past year as the trade in general took a downturn. With the threat of war looming and the possible consequences of bombing on the capital it was evidently prudent to evaluate their London assets. Therefore, in the spring of 1938 an inventory of the London office at St. Paul's Chambers, in Ludgate Hill was undertaken which provided a valuation of £569.8s.6d. It noted that the premises contained a telephone room, a general office, Mr A.W. Steele's office, and Mr R.F. Stileman's office.[22] In fact, a valuation for insurance purposes was taken of the entire premises owned by the Company. The financial assessment maintained that the relevant values were thus: Selwood buildings £73,000; Selwood plant £135,000; Adderwell Buildings £32,945; Adderwell plant £105,856; other properties £7,710; London office £749.[23]

As for the Selwood site at this point, the internal workings can be very clearly imagined thanks to an informative newspaper article which describes the premises in great detail. The article is undated but it must have been pre-war as the majority of processes were being undertaken at the Selwood works but were moved to Adderwell after the war.

Monotype Keyboards

On the stairway approach I caught the sound as of a pattering rain which swelled to a downpour as we entered the room where 26 machines were clattering away at the first stages of book production. The monotype is one of the results of the demand for speedier typesetting than the hand composition system offered. Its production rate being approximately seven times greater than that of a good compositor. The keyboard is the Grand Mogul of all typewriters carrying a multi-coloured bank of 225 keys on a stand surmounted by a complicated apparatus, among which can be discerned a reel of paper about 4 ins. wide. It represents one-half of an automatic typesetting mechanism and its function is to punch holes in the reel of paper which will ultimately operate the casting machine.

The depression of a key operates a series of connected levers which open compressed air valves the air pressure forcing up punches which pierce the paper. Each character has its own combination of punches and it is the position of the holes which determine the actions of the caster. The keyboard also works out and arranges automatically for the immense variation in spacing required to make every line of equal length – a function governed by a drum liberally covered with figures to which the operator refers at the end of each line. The speed of the lightning-fingered operators working from original copy is really remarkable.

The Ways of the Caster

The casting-room to which we next proceeded might be a musician's conception of inferno. It is noisy, to say the least, but its interest outweighs concern for the eardrums. Under the tutelage of Mr Newport I learned the ways of the caster, the more comprehensible parts of which are a metal pot, a mould, a square case of female dies representing the type characters. These dies are arranged in rows and the holes in the reel of paper offer a passage to compressed air which serves to bring the correct die over the mould, one hole determining the forward and backward movement of the die case and the other left to right action. Metal is pumped into the mould and the result is a perfect unit of type with the letter at the top ready for printing. These are assembled in lines and delivered and stacked automatically. The super caster is of a different pattern: it casts the rules and spacing material and also the larger letters used in display work. A silent and much more dignified machine than its near relation.

Contrast and an Obscure Species

As a contrast the first proof and reading department offered a cathedral-like silence. Here a proof is taken from the machine set type and passed to the readers for checking. Any necessary corrections are marked, inserted by compositors and the type and proofs go down to the main composing department. The readers are an obscure species hibernating in small cubicles from which can be heard faint incantations as the copy is read. Here labour the men who discharge the exacting business of picking the weeds from the typographical garden.

The composing room presented a neat arrangement of type-laden frames and racks of spacing and ornamental material. Under the supervision of Mr F. Dingle the compositors were engaged in separating the long columns of type into suitable lengths for pages, dropping in spaces and display types and securing each page by tying it round with cord. At this stage it is ready for the stone room. I believe the correct title is the 'Imposing' Department and here Mr Slade and his companions were preparing pages for printing and processing. The type pages are laid out on a steel surface (in earlier days a stone surface – hence the name) in correct order to allow of 16 pages being printed at once. Spaces are inserted for margins and the whole is wedged firmly into a rectangular frame by means of wedges – or speaking technically – they are 'locked up' in 'chases'. The type can then be lifted bodily without anxiety – up to this point it has called for the most careful handling.

It was at this stage that I learned that work is planned for as much as six weeks ahead and that it is possible within a fine margin of error to say what a particular press will be printing on any day within that period. An outstanding illustration of the house slogan 'Plan your work and work your plan' which is honoured by every unit of the staff.

A swift passage through its final reading dept – more enigmatic cubicles – and we entered the graveyards. I can think of no better name for those big rooms where thousands of tons of type in pages are stored after use, awaiting the call to service for a reprint. All stacked neatly in tiers, ticketed and filed for reference. These silent rooms were uncanny after the preceding hum of activity.

In the foundry I met Mr Ayres and his cohorts, who appear to be engineers, lead smiths, artists and chemists while they are about the business of giving a new form to type. They convert the type into flat plates for use on the presses, giving a more stable printing agent than loose type and providing an easy method for duplication. In one process, stereotyping, a mould is taken from the type on a steam press with a sheet of damp blotting-paper – at least, that's what it looks like – dries hard and gives a perfect reproduction. This paper matrix is placed in a casting box, metal is poured in a casting box, metal is poured in from a cauldron and the result is a plate having on one side a replica of the type surface.

Electrotyping

The plate is then trimmed and tonsured by clipping it into a contrivance resembling a miniature gas engine, which shaves the excess metal from the back: a second trim on a more compact apparatus and the plate is true to a thousandth of an inch.

The other method of type reproduction is electrotyping. A mould is taken from the type in wax, the mould carefully touched up with a fine brush and immersed in a bath of chemicals – under the treatment it takes on a coating of copper, and the thin copper shell corresponds in every particular to the original type. The shell is dropped on to a cauldron of molten metal which strengthens it and builds up the required thickness. It is then passed to the slabhand for levelling. This gentleman I understand is Craftsman No. 1 of the dept; upon his work hangs the perfection of the plate. It seemed difficult to believe for the said craftsman was laying on mightily on the back of the plate with hammer and punch.

The Final Stage

A return to ground level brought us to the machine room, the final stage in the preparation of the printed sheet. Here the many processes already noted are applied to paper and this highly spacious room appeared to bristle with machinery – small and speedy contrivances clicking away steadily, middle-weight presses in a variety of style and size and steel giants towering up to dwarf the men who clambered about them or burrowed into their inner parts. With the assistance of Mr Coles I absorbed some part of their complex operations, more particularly in the case of a battery of small machines some of which were printing a four-colour book jacket. As one colour was printed the sheet was passed on for the succeeding impressions until it had been through the stages of yellow, red, blue and black and, by overprinting these colours had taken on the original design of the artist in full colour. Not only did these machines ink and print, but they picked up the sheets, held them in the neatest fashion – and as a final service they sprayed the wet sheet with a fine coating of wax to assist the drying of the ink.

Mr Coles introduced me to the heavyweights too. These larger presses print as many as 128 pages of a book on one sheet in one revolution, feeding, printing and delivering a sheet 68 ins. by 45 ins. without any human assistance. From the pile of sheets at one end of the machine a row of suckers pick up the top sheet and take it forward to a number of travelling tapes which carry it down to a cylinder set across the reciprocating bed carrying the tape. The cylinder grips the sheet and revolves, pressing the sheet on to the inked type as the bed travels beneath. On its release from the cylinders the sheet runs on to delivery tapes which deposit it at the end of the machine.

Capable Young Ladies

Other presses, not quite so self-sufficient had the sheets fed by hand. This was done for them by a number of capable young ladies who looked much too small for the huge sheets they were handling but who nevertheless fed in steadily at 1,500 impressions an hour without a false move.

Reluctantly quitting this mechanical wonderland I passed on to the block storage rooms. Blocks are the things which print pictures – thin, copper plates mounted on wood. These have a habit of accumulating and Butler and Tanner must have thousands of them. There were hundreds of trays all filled to capacity in the room I saw and there are three more rooms of the same size directly below that one. And any block can be found in an instant so completely are they catalogued.

In parting, Mr Hillman casually mentioned a few trifles about the factory being equipped to produce its own power in the event of a service breakdown; that the entire building is guarded against fire by a sprinkler system sensitive to a lighted match.[24]

After almost a decade as Chairman of the Board, Humphrey was making some sound business decisions, advising on the purchasing of plant and machinery, making cost savings where appropriate and managing prices and industrial relations. He had proved himself a worthy leader thus far but greater challenges were ahead as Britain became embroiled into a conflict that was to last for years.

Endnotes

[1] S.H. Steinberg, Five Hundred Years of Printing, New edition rev. by John Trevitt, The British Library and Oak Knoll Press, London, 1996, p. 170.

[2] John Rhode, A Hundred Years of Printing: 1795–1895, Butler and Tanner Ltd, Frome and London, 1927, p. 75.

[3] Judith Slinn et al., History of the Monotype Corporation, Printing Historical Society, Vanbrugh Press, 2014, p. 376.

[4] Notes for Managing Directors Reports to Board of Directors of Butler and Tanner Ltd., The Selwood Printing Works, Frome. Butler and Tanner archive, Frome Museum, Frome, Somerset.

[5] Notice to employees on Butler and Tanner letterhead [undated], Butler and Tanner Archive, Frome Museum, Frome, Somerset.

6 Notes for Managing Directors Reports to Board of Directors of Butler and Tanner Ltd., The Selwood Printing Works, Frome. Butler and Tanner archive, Frome Museum, Frome, Somerset.

[7] *Ibid.*

[8] Interview with Steve Burry, 13th March, 2015.

[9] Notes for Managing Directors Reports to Board of Directors of Butler and Tanner Ltd., The Selwood Printing Works, Frome. Butler and Tanner archive, Frome Museum, Frome, Somerset.

[10] It is presumed that this was from George Mann & Co. Ltd, London manufacturers of offset lithography presses.

[11] Programme: Messrs. Butler and Tanner Ltd., Frome, Employees' Outing to the Thames and London, 6th July, 1929. Butler and Tanner Archive (DB4761/D7709), Frome Museum, Frome, Somerset.

[12] Programme: Employees' Outing to London and Brighton, 5th July, 1930. Butler and Tanner Archive (DB4761/D7709), Frome Museum, Frome, Somerset.

[13] Notes for Managing Directors Reports to Board of Directors of Butler and Tanner Ltd., The Selwood Printing Works, Frome. Butler and Tanner archive, Frome Museum, Frome, Somerset.

[14] An em is a typographic unit, traditionally the size of which is, the width of an uppercase letter 'M'.

[15] Notes for Managing Directors Reports to Board of Directors of Butler and Tanner Ltd., The Selwood Printing Works, Frome. Butler and Tanner archive, Frome Museum, Frome, Somerset.

[16] Interview with Mary Scott (Humphrey Tanner's daughter), 11th March, 2015.

[17] Notes for Managing Directors Reports to Board of Directors of Butler and Tanner Ltd., The Selwood Printing Works, Frome. Butler and Tanner archive, Frome Museum, Frome, Somerset.

[18] www.historypin.org [posted by Frome Society for Local Study] [site accessed 30th January, 2015]

[19] Notes for Managing Directors Reports to Board of Directors of Butler and Tanner Ltd., The Selwood Printing Works, Frome. Butler and Tanner archive, Frome Museum, Frome, Somerset.

[20] *Ibid.*

[21] *Ibid.*

[22] Inventory: Office Furniture, Fixtures and Fittings in London Office, 11th April, 1938, Frank Colebrook and Partners. Butler and Tanner Archive (DB5862/D9789), Frome Museum, Frome, Somerset.

[23] Valuation figures for full insurance purposes, 26th July, 1938, Butler and Tanner Archive (DB4774/D7832), Frome Museum, Frome, Somerset.

[24] 'In Search of Selwood: Being an Account of a Tour of the Printing Works of Messrs. Butler and Tanner', Somerset Standard, [undated], Butler and Tanner Archive (DB5039/D8489), Frome Museum, Frome

FIVE

The Difficult War Years and Beyond

The Second World War (1939 to 1945) impacted heavily upon the British printing and publishing trades. With the loss of employees due to both voluntary and, later, compulsory call-up to H.M. Forces or for other war work, staffing was to prove problematical. Additionally, paper shortages caused by the lack of such raw materials as esparto grass and wood pulp would severely affect the print industry. Paper rationing came into force regulated by the Paper Control Agency which, together with the Book Production War Economy Agreement prescribing the permissible size of type, width of margins, words per square inch, weight and quality of paper, would have affected Butler and Tanner as much as any other printer. However, there were also positive consequences for the trade when the 'demand for reading matter exceeded all previous records',[1] thus creating the need to print additional copies of books. Indeed, the national expenditure on books rose from £9 million in 1939 to £23 million in 1945.[2] Additionally, the government created print opportunities and such contracts were awarded throughout printing establishments, Butler and Tanner included.

The first hint of any intrusion into the Company's affairs, due to increasing political hostilities between Britain and Germany, came at a meeting of the Board on 16th June, 1938. Managing Director, Humphrey Russell Tanner, said 'I have given Air Raid Precautions considerable thought; but as I can get no information as to what cooperation they want out of those in authority I have not been able to do anything. I understand that in the near future a new A.R.P. Officer is to be appointed who proposes visiting the factories in the district.'[3] This was the precursor to a myriad of frustrations and difficulties he was to experience over the next eleven years; the stresses of which would accumulate to take a great toll upon his health.

By June 1939, world events were beginning to impact upon staffing decisions made by Butler and Tanner's directors, located as they were in rural Somerset, seemingly far away from such troubles on the continent. Guidelines issued by the Master Printers Federation (an organisation they had joined two years earlier) had recommended:

> That every facility possible be given to employees to join the Territorial Army or other Auxiliary Forces of the Crown.

> That any man joining should be granted two weeks leave of absence for training in 1939, his service pay and allowances being made up to his standard rate of pay and a week's holiday with pay being given in addition.

However, Humphrey Tanner's opinion was that the last clause (the week's holiday) was unnecessary and 'is not as far as I know, generally followed in Frome'.[4] This question of workers' holiday entitlement here being discussed in a pre-war context where the power balance was firmly in the favour of the Company owners, was later to undergo a significant shift in a post-war environment where workers' rights would be increasingly recognised. In fact, the recurring feature of all the Board Meetings throughout the years of the Second World War and its immediate aftermath, is that of increasing labour shortages and hence, rising wages. At the same meeting an application from the Readers Chapel requesting that Readers' minimum wage should be increased to 75*s.* per week from 68*s.*6*d.* This

Humphrey Russell Tanner

amount, they pointed out, would be the same as the Monotype keyboard operators. Humphrey recommended that this be paid as 'getting good readers was a problem'.[5] He also sought the Board's permission to install a new letterpress press (at a proposed cost of under £1,000) for the oddments of work still requiring this. The current machine, he explained, was thirty years old and it would not be cost effective to employ the newer, larger machines for the task of printing such small runs.

His philanthropic nature towards his individual employees is often shown in his discussions with the board to whom he recommends several cases. In one instance, in 1939, a request from one of their lorry drivers (two of his children had recently died after long and expensive illnesses), was made to the Company for a loan of £90 to be paid back at a rate of 20s. a week. The employee was prepared to deposit his life insurance policy for £100 as security so Humphrey could rest assured that they would not suffer any financial losses.

The impact of a country at war was soon felt within the printing trade. At a meeting on 11th December, 1939 Humphrey had the unenviable task of breaking some gloomy news to his fellow board members: 'on war breaking out we received instructions from most of our customers to stop work pending further instructions and for a fortnight things were very bad… things are generally a little better at the moment…the *AA Handbook* is definitely cancelled and *Holiday Haunts* is being produced in a reduced form.'[6] These two publications represented significant contracts for the Company and three new Smythe sewing machines (at a cost of £400 each) had been specifically put on order to help in the fulfilment of these. By June 1940, however, despite the fact that delivery had been taken of one machine, two others were provisionally cancelled. The cancelling of contracts was not the only problem caused by trading in a country at war. Initially, the impact of losing staff to the armed forces was not too great. In 1939, three staff members and a few Territorials from the Frome offices had gone to join the fight, although the London office was more seriously affected. By March 1940 three staff from the counting house and 25 from the works had joined the Armed Forces; whilst by August 1940 a total of 68 people from the works and four from the counting house had gone to fight for their country. However, by this stage losing staff was not the prime concern for the amount of work was decreasing alarmingly and they had advised members of staff to look for jobs elsewhere in the 'present conditions'.[7] Under the New Factory Act it was necessary to fit special guards to their platen machines. Two older machines were scrapped and replaced with one newer one as the cost of fitting guards to old machines was expensive and it didn't cost much more to purchase a new machine.

By the summer of 1940 real difficulties were beginning to affect the business as articulated by Humphrey when he reported that 'The paper position is at the moment the most difficult problem in connection with the trade. When war broke out paper was rationed at thirty per cent of normal requirements and I hear that there is a likelihood of its being further reduced possibly to ten per cent. It was chiefly this rationing that led to the cancelling of several of our larger contracts. At the moment we hold considerable stocks of paper, mostly on account of customers, which should keep us going for several months at present production; but when this is used up on the basis of ten per cent ration we shall only be working half a day a week.'[8]

Earlier in the war, in the spirit of national patriotism, the firm had decided to waive the allotment fees in view of the 'Dig for Victory' campaign. In this continuing vein of benevolence from the company and its staff, similar gestures included:

A display of fruit and vegetables at a Butler and Tanner horticultural show

a donation for £5.5s.6d. sent to the St John Ambulance Brigade; the introduction of a War Savings Committee and the implementation of a Red Cross Fund which raised about £5 per month. In later years a donation of £30.16s.0d. was given to the Frome Spitfire Fund donation.

A continuing theme throughout the years of the war was that while trading conditions in some cases worsened, in others financial opportunities resulting from circumstances brought about by the war were also to be gained. One such advantage was the greater demand for metal, which allowed Humphrey 'to sell some old rotary plates for £1,200'. On a similarly positive note he was able to report that, 'We are holding large stocks of binding materials such as cloth, straw boards, and glue and prices are hardening so I am hoping to see profit out of this. Publishers hold large stocks of sheets with us and owing to shortage of paper, are binding these up and selling them off, so I anticipate being busy in the binding department for some time'.[9] Due to increased transport rates at this time it was decided to ask customers to pay extra carriage to cover this. The question of whether they should arrange for the Adderwell works to be camouflaged was raised because, as he stated, 'How it stands up it can be seen from the top of Cley Hill.' Prices for doing the work were obtained. Once quotes for undertaking the work had been received to the amount of £495 it was decided not to proceed because 'surrounding buildings are not camouflaged'.[10]

Butler and Tanner's print works were situated in two major locations within Frome at the time. The typesetting, platemaking (except rotary plates) and printing departments were located in the Selwood Works at Trinity Street, and the bookbinding, rotary printing and rotary platemaking departments were situated at the Adderwell premises.[11] By the summer of 1940 Humphrey's greatest fear was that they may lose their Adderwell works under requisitioning laws, reporting to the Board that 'Officials of the Air Ministry recently came down to inspect our Adderwell works. I understand that they have complete powers to take it over if they wish to do so.'[12] This situation came about almost immediately; at the Board Meeting on 2nd August 1940 Humphrey gave the news to the rest of the group that 'the office of works have served a notice on us requisitioning most of our warehouse space at Adderwell. All this space contains customers' property not our own and I have not up to present been able to find out what our position is if the owners of the stock refuse to take delivery as there is no alternative accommodation in Frome. A large proportion is

printed sheets which in normal course of events we should bind, if sent away to be bound elsewhere lost sales would be £26,000. They 'are hoping that we may be able to get this requisition lifted.'[13]

Frome Local Defence Volunteers, including a platoon from Butler and Tanner

Additional financial implications directly applicable to wartime conditions were beginning to be felt by the firm. It was reported that Air Raid Precaution expenses up to September, 1939 had been £585.10s.2d and, up to July, a total of 2,636 hours had been lost due to air raid warnings representing a loss in wages of approximately £200. Additionally there was a requirement for a L.D.V. post and volunteers at Adderwell at the request of local authorities. Many employees joined platoons within the town and Butler and Tanner had its own platoon headed by Mr H. Topp.[14]

Business had worsened with only the '*Home Words* rotary' press running, sales were affected and salaries decreased: a situation deemed unsatisfactory but blamed upon the shortage of paper. By December 1940, the Ministry of Supply had taken over a warehouse at Adderwell despite efforts to try to get the requisition lifted. However, by rearranging other warehouses they were able to vacate without the need to rent any more space. All costs in connection with the upheaval were to be met by the Ministry and, by the summer of 1941, it had been agreed that the Air Ministry would pay £350 per annum rent for the warehouse at Adderwell. The main factory at Adderwell had also been inspected by the Ministry of Supply and various firms engaged in munitions thus prompting Humphrey to state, 'I consider it possible that at any time the whole place may be requisitioned.'[15]

From September a pay rise had been granted to employees in the printing trade – men up by 5 shillings a week, women by 2*s*.6*d*. and juveniles by 1*s*.6*d*. It was proposed that, in order to pay for this, prices to customers would have to rise by ten per cent for printing and five per cent for binding. On a

Aerial view of the Selwood Works with fire-watching point highlighted

more positive note the Board was informed that the centre for air raid warnings had recently moved from Bristol to Yeovil so that the alerts were becoming fewer. In addition, by registering with the authorities under the Purchase Tax rules, they were able to buy materials used in the manufacture of books free of tax. However, in order to do so they could only be ordered and signed for by a Director or duly authorised person. As with other businesses, Butler and Tanner was continuously being issued with instructions from the Ministry of Labour to undertake various initiatives all of which cost money and upon which they would get no return. For example, they had to employ people as fire watchers whose wages were an additional overhead incurred with no production to warrant it. Fire watching entailed the appointed leader, William Pobjoy, having to create duty rosters and to be trained in fire fighting and the use of motor fire pumps. Additionally, he was required to learn how to deal with incendiary bombs should the need arise and to train any necessary fire watching personnel. The work was tiring when carried out in addition to normal working hours. A Ministry official suggested that Butler and Tanner's employees should do more to help with the war effort, thus arranging for them to provide assistance at a milk factory. With some staff working evenings and weekends packing powdered milk,

Humphrey Tanner and William Pobjoy undertook the boiler stoker's duties on Friday and Saturday nights.[16] Other measures they would also have to comply with included the new Glass (Factories Protection Order) 1940 whereby all the glass had to be protected against blast by wire netting or something similar. However, as a non-priority industry it was feared that materials might be difficult to come by and that costs would be considerable. The government's new Act of Compulsory Insurance for air raid damage was to cost Butler and Tanner over £4,500 per year. By 1941 air raid shelters had been built to comply with government regulations at a cost to the firm of £439.10s.0d., and fire-watching, raid spotters and warnings had cost £881.7s.11d.

Transportation problems also hampered the business when the railways refused to accept goods traffic and road transport became increasingly irregular. Staff members continued to leave the firm in order to join H.M. Forces but with less overall business there was less work to occupy them in any event.

In March 1941 the whole of the Adderwell Works were taken over by the Ministry of Aircraft Production and by 2nd April Butler and Tanner had ceased production there. The company of J. Evans & Son (Portsmouth) Ltd. was installed in the premises and keen to have access to as much of the space as possible. In a letter to Butler and Tanner they wrote, 'Under the powers of the above order, please take notice that the spaces which we require are to be cleared quickly at all costs even if it means that the paper which is a serious obstruction has to be dumped in the open.'[17] The publishers' stock to the value of £250,000 had been cleared out but there was more to be rid of and an acceptable rate for the rental of the premises had yet to be agreed with the Ministry. All machinery was promptly removed with the exception of the largest printing machines which, if they were to be put in the open it was to be at Butler and Tanner's risk. The only option was to sell them and they had already had some interest. One potential purchaser from Canada wanted to buy a complete plant. Some of the modern bindery plant was sent to Pitmans in Bath and operatives travelled there daily to work; finances for this were still to be discussed.

Initially Pitmans paid the wages of £90 per week and Butler and Tanner paid travelling costs of £20 per week.

By the end of 1941 there were general wage rises across the printing industry so Butler and Tanner's directors also proposed an increase for their staff. In addition, higher wages were being offered in town for other occupations so Humphrey proposed that 'those who stick by us should be rewarded'.[18] With less printing work to be done the Company rented out some of its machinery to two other printing firms: Clay and Son and Purnell and Son at a rate of fifteen per cent per annum on the capital value of machines plus insurance charges. Their premises had been in great demand since the beginning of the war and this was set to continue. The Admiralty informed Butler and Tanner that they would be taking over 6,000 square feet for storage purposes. In a letter dated 10th January, 1942 from H.M.S.O. London the proposal to take part of factory for storage was confirmed in no uncertain terms: 'Contract for supply of Admiralty Pilot books cannot be hindered. The space is ultimately requisitioned for the execution of Stationery Office work.'[19]

In 1943, it was a relief to Humphrey when he received a letter from the Ministry of Aircraft Production informing them that they didn't have to move the larger machines from the works premises at Adderwell. This glimmer of good news was counteracted, however, by the very grim news that Mr A.W. Steele from the London office had been reported as a prisoner of war in Japan. The principal challenge during this period was the withdrawal of labour, in addition to which the factory took on weekend shifts to pack voluntarily milk for the Ministry of Food. With the loss of male staff members women were an increasing source of labour and the National Arbitration Board granted wage increase to women of four shillings a week to a wage of £15 per week. An additional annoyance was that the Regional Petroleum Officer had refused to renew the petrol permit for Humphrey's business purposes. By the end of 1943 there had been another wage rise of an extra 7*s*.6*d*. per week for men and 3*s*. for women. By the beginning of 1944, to counteract the rise in wages, it was agreed that they would increase their prices to customers by 7.5 per cent for printing and five per cent for binding. A small positive step in the trade was that the paper quota for book publishers had recently increased by 2.5 per cent.

The frustrations felt by those running the Company during the war manifested themselves in many ways: one such issue occurred in 1944 when the Ministry of Trade instructed them to reduce power consumption by fifteen per cent but at the same time the Ministry of Labour told them to work a standard 56 instead of 45 hours per week. Humphrey was able to report to the Board, however, that, 'In view of the difficulties these schemes seem to have died a death.' There were, however, advantages to be gained by businesses throughout the war years and one positive outcome was securing printing work from the government and, in 1944, Butler and Tanner obtained another contract from H.M.S.O. and one for the Ministry of Aircraft Production which as Humphrey cheerfully reported, 'Having these helps considerably when the Ministry of Labour try to take people away from us.'[20]

Thoughts began to turn toward the ending of the war and positive plans for the future of the business were beginning to be put in place by the end of 1944. Humphrey was happy to announce to the Board that they would start migration from Selwood to Adderwell, subject to them being able to settle reasonable terms with the Ministry of Aircraft Production. The Selwood premises, having been built in 1870, required a great deal of repair works and by using it solely for warehousing allowed them to dispose of all the other small warehouses scattered around the town.[21] One advantage of having had the buildings at Adderwell requisitioned was that heating, lighting and new floors had been installed. Humphrey was very keen to get the things moving and planned to develop the offset department. He endeavoured to get the Board of Trade to hurry up the Ministry of Aircraft Production on the grounds that they produced quite a few catalogues for export. In an effort to make sure that business could get moving once again they approached several of their former employees to ask them to return to Butler and Tanner.[22]

Additionally, meetings were held with the Board of Trade and the Ministry of Labour in an attempt at getting staff released.

In 1945 they purchased the old offices of the *Somerset and Wilts. Journal* for the sum of £2,500 in order to secure storage space for white paper. Immediate post-war optimism meant trade was good and the firm's presses were fully booked for six months ahead and they had to turn down work. The release of the Adderwell works was happening much too slowly for Humphrey's liking: he made frequent applications to authorities to get Adderwell back but obtaining only the responses that it was 'under consideration'. He feared the possibility that the premises would be required for the manufacture of parts for prefabricated homes in which case he reported, 'it will be impossible to say when we should get possession.'[23]

Just before the start of the war one of their German customers had ordered the printing of some books (either encyclopaedias or dictionaries) to be bound in leather. However, upon declaration of hostilities between the two countries all such shipping was cancelled. Butler and Tanner, therefore, duly stored the books in a cellar until after the war when they managed to send them to their German customer. In gratitude for this kindness, they were presented with the gift of a clock.[24]

There was a legal obligation upon companies to employ those staff members returning from the Forces and Butler and Tanner complied with this but it was imperative that the Adderwell premises were returned to them so that they could not only fulfil the orders but fully occupy those returning employees. However, by the end of 1945 this still had not happened. Humphrey was pleased to announce that 'Major Steele (London representative) was back from being a prisoner of war in 'Japanese hands' and hoped to be back to work by end of January'.[25] Finally, by the summer of 1946, part of the Adderwell factory had been derequisitioned. Butler and Tanner had come to an agreement that they would pay a fee for betterment to the Ministry of Aircraft Production of approximately

£7,000. This is to pay for the improvement works undertaken which included new offices, an enlarged canteen, cement floors and heating in warehouses which enabled the offset department to move out of the main factory.[26]

Humphrey Tanner, by this time, was feeling the strain of the last six years and on medical advice asked the Board to relieve him of his position as Secretary of the Company and suggested that Mr C.C. Flemming should be appointed to the office at a salary of £1,250 per annum and also to assume the position of Assistant Managing Director. He reported that the future seemed uncertain and, whilst there was 'plenty of work, the Trade Unions are demanding a 40 hour week instead of a 45 hour week and a fortnight's holiday with pay'.[27] The Master Printers Federation offered the holiday and 43.5 hour week but this was turned down and an embargo placed on overtime and a ballot held for strike action. A casualty of the war had been the loss of the long running contract to print the *Home Words* magazine.

Finally, by the beginning of 1947 the Adderwell premises were up and running with costs to be eventually repaid by the Ministry. Unions and Master Printers had agreed to cut working hours to 43.5 hours, 14 days holiday from seven days and an increase in wages for journeymen of 10*s.* a week. These costs were passed on to customers with twenty per cent price increase, Humphrey reporting that, 'so far few publishers have squealed'.[28]

Humphrey had been giving thought to the post-war future of the Company, giving consideration to its status, 'I think the time has come when we should consider becoming a Public instead of a Private company. People, both company lawyers, stock brokers and businessmen with whom I have discussed the matter in the abstract in London are unanimously of the opinion that the days of the family business, specially the larger ones, are over. Becoming a public company would not necessarily mean that we had to dispose of any shares but would put us in a position to do so if we wished i.e. for payment of death duties etc. I do not think the Treasury would accept our balance sheet capital of £80,000 in view of the fact that our 1938 valuation of our plant and machinery alone was over £300,000.'[29] Humphrey began to assess the possible problems going forward. He reported to the Board that, 'Our chief difficulty in the near future is going to be getting materials specifically for binding. We are already getting letters from manufacturers saying they will have to put us on a quarter of what we used in 1939.'[30] By the summer of 1947 they were still attempting to claim £10,000 from the Ministry of Supply.

An architect's report showed the Selwood premises to be in a very bad state and not repairable. Therefore, a decision was made to move immediately all the type metal and heavy machinery to the Adderwell premises. Two rotary presses were moved to Adderwell and they aimed to sell a German machine which was only being used for a couple of weeks a year. In addition the machines bought to print *Home Words* were also to be disposed of. The contract for printing this journal had effectively ceased when the premises were requisitioned.[31] In view of the precarious power position, they ordered new diesel generating plant at a cost of £4,400 to allow the Adderwell works to be independent of the town supply of electricity. Once installed, in 1948, it was used every Tuesday as agreed with the local electricity supply company; the general move to Adderwell proceeding as and when licences had been granted to them.

By 1948 a final agreement had been made with the Ministry of Supply over damages to Adderwell done by Evans and Sons to the value of £12,000 and the betterment fee (i.e. the amount owing by Butler and Tanner for the improvements) at £6,500. The Selwood premises had been vacated and Butler and Tanner were endeavouring to dispose of them. Having applied to the council for a permit to build they hoped to address the housing issue which they believed was one of the chief causes of labour difficulties. Humphrey's opinions on government intervention and his sense of annoyance at such interference is clearly demonstrated when he reported to the Board, 'In view of the wish informed by the powers that be that all companies of any size should have a woman liaison officer we have appointed Mrs Flemming to this post at a salary of £250 per annum. So far this arrangement has proved excellent and much better than having to take someone appointed by Whitehall.' [32]

Joseph Russell Tanner joined the family business in 1948 having studied on a two-year course at the London School of Printing. Embarking upon his apprenticeship at Frome, he learned his trade firstly with the compositors, followed by time spent in the machine-room and the bindery.[33] According to Joseph's sister, however, he hadn't wanted to go into the family business preferring to take an altogether different job and had to be persuaded to carry on the family tradition.[34]

By the beginning of 1949 they were still awaiting the settlement from the Ministry of Supply. Having installed their own generator for use on Tuesdays and Fridays, they were able to solve the problem of power cuts. With the government's requisition of their Adderwell premises, Butler and Tanner had been obliged to move their plant back to the Selwood premises and to carry on their business from there for many years. In their absence part of the Adderwell site had been taken over by the engineering company, J.E. Evans. They had been evacuated from Portsmouth to Frome and at the peak of production there were 800 workers employed in the task of manufacturing aircraft components for the war effort, such as glider undercarriages and bomb containers. Visitors to the requisitioned premises during the War included Queen Mary and, the Minister of Aircraft Production, Sir Stafford Cripps.

The BBC recorded several 'Workers Playtime' concert parties at the premises. All performers were factory workers and the lunchtime concerts presented to their fellow workers and aired live on BBC radio. Boxing evenings were also held at the factory and one dinner guest of honour was Jimmy Wilde who had been World Flyweight Champion in 1916. Some local women had been drafted for war work at Evans and indeed some of Butler and Tanner's own employees were transferred to such war work. Only three bombs fell on Frome during the war but one killed an air raid warden.[35]

In April 1949 Humphrey Russell Tanner retired from his post as Managing Director. He did, however, retain his position as Chairman until his death in October 1950. It was in 1949 that they first produced a newsletter for members of staff. In the first edition its purpose was explained: 'This Newsletter has been inaugurated so that everyone in the firm may know what is going on. Many of us can see only what is happening in our own department; we do not know what is taking place next door, what is being planned for the future, what happens to our work when it leaves us, or who outside the firm is interested in us. It is hoped that by filling some of these gaps our occupations will become more interesting.'[36] It is evident from this publication that a multitude of social pursuits were engaged upon by staff members: flower show participation; dances; Christmas parties for children of staff; cricket teams; hockey matches; rifle shooting; snooker; swimming; table tennis and skittles all of which were continued over a period of many decades. In fact, in the 1960s there was a Motor Club and even a Butler and Tanner U.F.O. Society.

An entry in the first edition confirmed that Mr R.F. Stilman who had been in charge of the London office since 1936 had resigned due to disability caused by a broken leg having been knocked down by a bus. His replacement was a Mr D.K.C. Dickens who was the great-grandson of the author Charles Dickens who spent nine months at Frome in various departments learning about all aspects of the business before taking up his position in the London office.[37] However, he subsequently left Butler and Tanner to run Pitman's publishing company.[38]

A summary of the situation with the Adderwell premises was laid out before staff. By 1939 the warehouses had been finished on the Adderwell site, and the ground works completed but the new factory remained unbuilt and the offices were equally absent. Subsequent requisitioning by the Ministry of Aircraft Production had resulted in the siting of four huts upon these ground works as well as the building of offices. Therefore, it was planned that the move to Adderwell would be made as soon as the site was derequisitioned. Thus, by 1949 the bindery, machine room, foundry and all the presses (except for the older machines) had been transferred to the new site. Additional building was necessary and planned but the required permits from the Board of Trade were slow to emerge.

In 1950 the Company introduced a contributory pension scheme for its members of staff. In the same year it formed a lending library for staff to borrow books and magazines (a librarian being available to provide the service on Monday and Friday lunchtimes in the canteen). A meeting between the firm's management and union representatives commenced discussion on the possibility of introducing an incentive scheme for employees.[39]

The death of Humphrey Russell Tanner on 4th October, 1950 was reported in the staff newsletter. His strong personality and dry wit are evident from the notes he wrote in preparation for board meetings. However, there are a couple of anecdotes that provide an even greater insight into his personality. Allegedly, at one particular town meeting when his presence was objected to, Humphrey Tanner's quick-witted response to such heckling had been, 'Well, I do know that it takes six pennies to make just one tanner.' On another occasion when enjoying a meal at the George Hotel, a wine waiter approached to ask Humphrey to choose the accompaniment to the fish course of his meal. Humphrey's reply of 'whiskey' caused the affronted waiter to blanch and step back with disdain to which Humphrey retorted, 'My dear young man, I've been having whiskey with my fish since before you were born.'[40] Humphrey Tanner's leadership throughout the war years had allowed the business to survive and, ultimately, thrive.

Endnotes

[1] S.H. Steinberg, *Five Hundred Years of Printing*, New edition rev. by John Trevitt, The British Library and Oak Knoll Press, London, 1996, p. 199.

[2] Robert Hewison, *Under Siege: Literary Life in London, 1939–1945* (London: Weidenfeld & Nicholson, 1977), p. 86.

[3] 'Notes for Managing Directors Reports to Board of Directors of Butler and Tanner Ltd, The Selwood Printing Works, Frome', Butler and Tanner Archive, Frome Museum, Frome, Somerset.

[4] *Ibid.*

[5] *Ibid.*

[6] *Ibid.*

[7] *Ibid.*

[8] *Ibid.*

[9] *Ibid.*

[10] *Ibid.*

[11] *The Butler and Tanner Group Newsletter*, Issue No. 21, October 2000, p. 44.

[12] Notes for Managing Directors Reports to Board of Directors of Butler and Tanner Ltd, The Selwood Printing Works, Frome, Butler and Tanner Archive, Frome Museum, Frome, Somerset.

[13] *Ibid.*

[14] *The Butler and Tanner Group Newsletter*, Issue No. 21, October 2000, p. 45.

[15] Notes for Managing Directors Reports to Board of Directors of Butler and Tanner Ltd, The Selwood Printing Works, Frome, Butler and Tanner Archive, Frome Museum, Frome, Somerset.

[16] *The Butler and Tanner Group Newsletter*, Issue No. 21, October 2000, p. 46.

[17] Letter from J. Evans & Son (Portsmouth) Ltd, Requisitioning order No. 41/W6(c), for and on behalf of the Minister of Aircraft Production, 17th March, 1941. Butler and Tanner Archive, Frome Museum, Frome, Somerset.

[18] Notes for Managing Directors Reports to Board of Directors of Butler and Tanner Ltd, The Selwood Printing Works, Frome, Butler and Tanner Archive, Frome Museum, Frome, Somerset.

[19] Letter from H.M.S.O. London, 10th January, 1942.

[20] Notes for Managing Directors Reports to Board of Directors of Butler and Tanner Ltd, The Selwood Printing Works, Frome, Butler and Tanner Archive, Frome Museum, Frome, Somerset.

[21] *Ibid.*

[22] *Ibid.*

[23] *Ibid.*

[24] Interview with Mary Scott (Humphrey Tanner's daughter), 11th March, 2015.

[25] Notes for Managing Directors Reports to Board of Directors of Butler and Tanner Ltd, The Selwood Printing Works, Frome, Butler and Tanner Archive, Frome Museum, Frome, Somerset.

[26] *Ibid.*

[27] *Ibid.*

[28] *Ibid.*

[29] *Ibid.*

[30] *Ibid.*

[31] *Ibid.*

[32] *Ibid.*

[33] Obituary: Joe Tanner, *The Independent*, 29th April 2006.

[34] Interview with Mary Scott (Joseph Tanner's sister), 11th March, 2015.

[35] *Working Memories: Frome Workers tell their Stories Home in* Frome in association with Millstream Books, Frome 2012, pp. 128–130.

[36] *The Newsletter: Journal of the House of Butler & Tanner Ltd.*, No.1 November–December 1949, Butler and Tanner, Frome, p. 1.

[37] *The Newsletter: Journal of the House of Butler & Tanner Ltd.*, No.4 May–June 1950, Butler and Tanner, Frome, p. 1.

[38] *Newsletter: Journal of the House of Butler and Tanner Ltd.*, No. 141, Summer 1973, pp. 9–10.

[39] *The Newsletter: Journal of the House of Butler & Tanner Ltd.*, No.4 May–June 1950, Butler and Tanner, Frome, p. 4.

[40] Interview with Mary Scott (Humphrey Tanner's daughter), 11th March, 2015.

SIX

Post-war Change and Growth

Butler and Tanner's last ever piece of printed matter using movable type

Before the middle of the twentieth century the vast majority of books were printed by letterpress with only a very few being manufactured by offset lithography, photogravure or collotype. During the second half of the twentieth century, however, book production changed radically.[1] Post-war advances in phototypesetting and offset lithography would, ultimately, consign hot metal type and letterpress printing to the past. Butler and Tanner's eventual closing of the letterpress section entailed the scrapping of twenty machines, 915 tons of metal and more than 60,000 'pi-mats'.[2]

With the retirement and subsequent death of Humphrey Tanner, the Managing Director's role was fulfilled by Captain C.C. Flemming. Although the war had been over for four years, conditions in which to run a business had not returned to normal. There continued to be paper shortages and a coal rationing, both of which adversely affected the business. In addition, with the introduction of National Service male members of staff continued to leave to join the Forces and women still gave up their positions upon marriage. However, the standard of workmanship remained high within the Company: it is noticeable

An early photo-typesetting matrix

Captain C.C. Flemming

that they received many letters from extremely satisfied customers and very infrequently ones complaining of mistakes, although on the rare occasion that this did occur, staff were left in no doubt of the severity of this and the costs incurred.

By the end of 1950 it was evident that there was a worldwide shortage of paper and members of staff were asked to avoid any wastage. The situation regarding cylinder sheets was 'as bad as during the War.'[3] The paper shortage gave rise to a 'Save Paper Campaign' whereby paper was collected for recycling with paper mills paying £6.10s. per ton for any waste paper collected. Butler and Tanner' s employees were urged to participate by bringing to the factory any waste paper; with any money raised being donated to the staff benevolent fund and sick club.[4] The response, it was subsequently reported, was 'very good', however, temptation became too much for one employee who stole bundles of *The Beano* comic, *Picture Post* and *Everybody's*.[5]

Even though post-war supplies of paper had grown, demand outstripped supply and there remained a shortage of paper and cardboard greater than that experienced throughout the years of the Second World War. Paper material sources in post-war Britain comprised fifty-seven per cent wood, pulp and pulp wood, eleven per cent esparto, rags and straw and thirty-two per cent recycled waste paper.[6] By the summer of 1951 the Butler and Tanner paper recycling effort was going well but the target of collecting a total of two-and-a-half tons had not yet been met. The price being paid by this time was £16 per ton.[7] At the beginning of 1952 the collections were managing prices of £20 per ton for newspapers and £16 per ton for all other waste paper – a sign of the increasing shortage of paper in the country.[8] The paper crisis may have eased by the summer of 1952 as the price had dropped to £12.10s. per ton.[9] This situation improved until the paper cost fell to £9 10s.per ton by the beginning of 1954.[10] Butler and Tanner continued to collect paper for recycling for many decades, putting the money acquired to good use. Twenty years later they were still able to command a good price for their salvage paper for the price had risen to £25 per ton by that time.[11] Coal was also still being rationed and the firm's allocation by the Ministry of Fuel and Power for the winter of 1951 to 1952 was reduced by five tons a week on the previous winter.[12] With his naval connections, Captain Flemming purchased two generators previously used aboard ship, in order to assist with the generating of their electricity.[13] The tall factory chimney on the Adderwell site was, apparently, kept clean by burning oily rags and the ashes from coal fires used to create building blocks, evidently prior to concerns about potential damaging emissions.[14]

Many employees worked for the Company for a substantial number of years. It was not unusual for those retiring to have worked at Butler and Tanner for more than half a century. In the spring of 1952 their oldest employee finally retired at the age of 78. Miss Hetty Dicks had worked for them for 65 years in the F.C.D (Folding and Collating Department).[15] She suffered from painful, swollen legs and it is remembered that she sat at work with paper and calico wrapped with tape around them.[16] In fact, several ladies, believed to have been in their eighties, still working in the factory, wore slippers with holes cut out of them to accommodate their bunions. [17] Women were primarily employed in the bindery and the F.C.D. Former employees of the period remember their overseer, a Mr Turk, walking around the areas where the female workers were employed holding a contraption which 'squirted disinfectant which stung their eyes'. This was to cut down on the spread of germs, hence to lesson instances of common illnesses easily caught in the workplace, thus, ensuring less absenteeism.[18] The female workers were forbidden from perusing the medical textbooks and, when the firm printed copies of the formerly banned *Lady Chatterley's Lover* they were most certainly not allowed to read that.[19] With the company working three shifts to keep up production, it was a lady called Jean Hicks who was the first female worker to undertake the night shift which, she apparently enjoyed.[20] Staff members were obliged to 'clock in' and were fined a penny (whether for each minute or a longer period it isn't remembered) with all such monies collected going to the charitable cause of the town's Victoria Hospital.[21] While there was much loyalty to the firm, maintaining staffing levels following those losses from the war years was an issue to be considered by those running the business: with young men leaving to undertake their compulsory National Service and young women continuing to leave upon marriage, it was essential to source new workers. A recruitment drive was deemed necessary and an open day organised whereby local schools were invited to send pupils with their parents to consider the kinds of jobs on offer within the print works. This was to become a regular feature 'held in an effort to interest the best young people around Frome in printing as a career.'[22]

The Company's accident record had generally been good over the years, in an industry generally considered to have its fair share of perils. The working environment in the printing and book production trade was one where losing a finger could be considered an occupational hazard. Aside from the terrible fatal accident in 1927, there had been few

serious mishaps during the first half of the twentieth century. However, in 1950 one such incident was recorded whereby a Mr D. Chivers, working in the machine room, fell from a laying-on board and fractured his shoulder. First aid was given and he was taken to hospital.[23]

A drum-cylinder press built by the Babcock Printing Press

The move from Selwood to Adderwell was almost complete when the Monotype Composing Department was finally transferred. The only remaining components to undertake the move were the 'Block' and 'Composing' stores. Although reportedly slow, two Babcock drum-cylinder presses were still in use in the 1950s for 'make ready'.

The Butler and Tanner workers were a sociable crowd and the Christmas of 1952 saw each department celebrate in their own manner. In the Bindery the Christmas spirit could be seen in abundance with the 'time-honoured custom of 'chasing' was observed and the usual reward under the mistletoe claimed… …After a while it was noticed however that very few needed to be chased and some really first-class clinches were witnessed.'[24]

Whilst the 1950s enjoyed a 'minor boom in the printing industry', Flemming explained to staff that Butler and Tanner were failing to enjoy its benefits; partly because of growing competition from Dutch, Belgian and German printers but also because Butler and Tanner were failing to keep up with orders due to a bottleneck in the composing department. He explained that even though staff numbers were eighty-one per cent of the pre-war period output was only sixty-seven per cent of what it had been.[25] A pay performance structure was introduced whereby employee's output was measured and targets set which, if met could earn a bonus for that staff member. However, this was initially met with much opposition. Recruitment in the Machine Room was proving to be troublesome since many of the men were of retirement age and extensive advertising had failed to obtain any skilled labour. Only five apprentices had been allowed to join the firm's machine room [by the Union, presumably] and 18 of the 39 employees in that

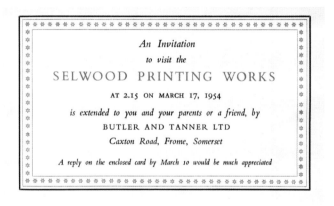

An Invitation
to visit the
SELWOOD PRINTING WORKS
AT 2.15 ON MARCH 17, 1954
is extended to you and your parents or a friend, by
BUTLER AND TANNER LTD
Caxton Road, Frome, Somerset

A reply on the enclosed card by March 10 would be much appreciated

Part of a recruitment drive, a 1954 invitation to visit Butler and Tanner

department were over the age of 59.[26] An open day with formal invitations was arranged to encourage recruitment. Supply and demand in the labour market affected wages and, by 1956, it was reported to the board that wage increases were now costing £1,000 more each week than the previous year.[27]

As with all families there were sad events as well as those to be celebrated. In December 1954, Ellen Tanner (Lanfear's wife and Donald's mother) had died. She had been on the board of directors when the partnership had been incorporated as a limited company more than thirty years previously.[28] The younger generations of the family were celebrating happier events, however. Having been elected director earlier in the year, in September

1956 Joseph Russell Tanner (great-grandson of the firm's founder) married Fenella Flemming (daughter of Captain C.C. Flemming).[29] They were to have four children: Christopher, Thomas, Amanda and Jeremy. Christopher was to follow his father into the printing trade and began his apprenticeship within the print works. However, he was sadly killed in a car crash in his early twenties. A games room at the Company's social club was subsequently named 'The Chris Tanner Room' in his honour. Neither of the remaining siblings chose to go into the printing business and thus, Joseph was to be the last Tanner to continue the family legacy.

An aerial view of the Adderwell works taken in 1959

In 1959 the country's printers went out on strike for seven weeks thus only apprentices and overseers were allowed to run the presses at Butler and Tanner during that period.[30] An aerial photograph, taken in 1959, shows the extent of the Adderwell premises. Part of the roof had been removed (a) to allow for the installation of the Bristolian Rotary Press in 1960. The steel framework was the structure for a new building (b) which was ultimately used as maintenance workshops. The central open area (c) is the site where a new building would be built (c. 1961) to accommodate the offset mono print room. Old air-raid shelters are located by the roadway separating the main road and warehouses (d) and another legacy from the war years, old Seco huts and cycle shed (e) which had been constructed by Evans Engineering during their period of occupation. Butler and Tanner allotments can be seen in the foreground; these had been particularly useful during the Dig for Victory campaign.[31] Their premises' proximity to the railway can clearly be seen.

By 1960 Butler and Tanner had more orders than they were able to cope with due to lack of skilled labour, a situation attributed in part to lack of housing availability.[32] They already owned some domestic properties in the town which they let to employees, including the cottages at Caxton Road. The tenants at 1, Caxton Road were the Bowden family and they remember that 'Mr Humphrey used to bring down pots of paint for the house, in a battleship grey colour.'[33] The purchase of the Easthill estate, for £6,400 in 1960 with the object of using the houses as transit accommodation, proved untenable as the cost of rents was controlled by government and were too low.[34] However, they retained the houses until 1987 when they sold them at a profit, for £156,576.[35]

It was during this boom period that Joseph Russell Tanner was to become Managing Director: the business was moving into its fourth generation of family ownership.

Endnotes

[1] *S.H. Steinberg, Five Hundred Years of Printing*, New edn., rev. by John Trevitt, The British Library and Oak Knoll Press, London, 1996 p. 218.
[2] Joseph Tanner, 'A Selwood Scrapbook', p. 76a [unpublished notes], Butler and Tanner Archive (DB5884/L2692), Frome, Somerset.
[3] *The Newsletter: Journal of the House of Butler & Tanner Ltd.*, No.6 September–October 1950, Butler and Tanner, Frome, p. 1.
[4] *The Newsletter: Journal of the House of Butler & Tanner Ltd.*, No. 9 March–April 1951, Butler and Tanner, Frome, p. 6.
[5] *The Newsletter: Journal of the House of Butler & Tanner Ltd.*, No. 10 May–June 1951, Butler and Tanner, Frome, p. 1.
[6] *The Newsletter: Journal of the House of Butler & Tanner Ltd.*, No. 11 July–August 1951, Butler and Tanner, Frome, p. 1.
[7] *Ibid.*
[8] *The Newsletter: Journal of the House of Butler & Tanner Ltd.*, No. 13 November–December 1951, Butler and Tanner, Frome, p. 2.
[9] *The Newsletter: Journal of the House of Butler & Tanner Ltd.*, No. 13 May–June 1952, Butler and

Tanner, Frome, p. 2.

[10] *The Newsletter: Journal of the House of Butler & Tanner Ltd.*, No. 26 January–February 1954, Butler and Tanner, Frome, p. 9.

[11] *Newsletter: Journal of the House of Butler and Tanner Ltd.*, Autumn 1974, p. 8.

[12] *The Newsletter: Journal of the House of Butler & Tanner Ltd.*, No. 13 November–December 1951, Butler and Tanner, Frome, p. 10.

[13] Interview with David Bowden, 13th March, 2015.

[14] *Ibid.*

[15] *The Newsletter: Journal of the House of Butler & Tanner Ltd.*, No. 15 March–April 1951, Butler and Tanner, Frome, p. 5.

[16] Interview with Sally Bowden and Jean Hicks, 13th March, 2015.

[17] Interview with Marion Lucas, 13th March, 2015.

[18] Interview with Sally Bowden and Jean Hicks, 13th March, 2015.

[19] *Ibid.*

[20] Interview with Jean Hicks, 13th March, 2015.

[21] Interview with Sally Bowden, 13th March 2015.

[22] *The Newsletter: Journal of the House of Butler & Tanner Ltd.*, No. 28 May–June 1954, Butler and Tanner, Frome, p. 5.

[23] *The Newsletter: Journal of the House of Butler & Tanner Ltd.*, No.7 November–December 1950, Butler and Tanner, Frome, p. 2.

[24] *The Newsletter: Journal of the House of Butler & Tanner Ltd.*, No.26 January–February 1954, Butler and Tanner, Frome, p. 1.

[25] *The Newsletter: Journal of the House of Butler & Tanner Ltd.*, No. 29 July–August 1954, Butler and Tanner, Frome, p. 4.

[26] *The Newsletter: Journal of the House of Butler & Tanner Ltd.*, No. 37 November–December 1955, Butler and Tanner, Frome, p. 6.

[27] *The Newsletter: Journal of the House of Butler & Tanner Ltd.*, No. 41 July–August 1956, Butler and Tanner, Frome, p. 3.

[28] *The Newsletter: Journal of the House of Butler & Tanner Ltd.*, No. 32 January–February 1955, Butler and Tanner, Frome, p. 3.

[29] *The Newsletter: Journal of the House of Butler & Tanner Ltd.*, No. 42 September–October 1956, Butler and Tanner, Frome, p. 1.

[30] Roger Clark, *The Butler and Tanner Group Newsletter*, Issue 9, February 2000, pp. 41–43.

[31] Harry Hallet, *The Butler and Tanner Group Newsletter*, Issue 10, February 1997, p. 26.

[32] *The Newsletter: Journal of the House of Butler & Tanner Ltd.*, No. 62, March–April 1960, Butler and Tanner, Frome, p. 6.

[33] Interview with Sally and David Bowden, 13th March, 2015.

[34] Joseph Tanner, 'A Selwood Scrapbook', [unpublished notes], Butler and Tanner Archive (DB5884/L2692), Frome, Somerset.

[35] *Ibid.*

SEVEN

Joseph Russell Tanner

Joseph Russell Tanner,
affectionately known as 'Mr Joe'

Rapid advances in post-war technology, primarily those associated with phototypesetting and offset lithography, would transform the printing industry over the following decades. Composition and typesetting underwent something of a revolution when it became possible for text to be made ready for printing either by film for direct exposure onto the printing plate or as an image on paper to be photographed.[1] Offset lithography proved advantageous, especially web offset, where paper could be delivered to the press from a reel and after printing, split into ribbons for ease of folding and integration into automated binding lines.[2] Butler and Tanner remained at the forefront in their implementation of such technology.

In 1964, Joseph Russell Tanner, great-grandson of the firm's original Joseph Tanner, became Managing Director and, after six years, took on the role of Chairman. He was to head the Company for thirty years until his retirement, maintaining an interest in the business and his colleagues long after, frequently calling in for a chat. In the first year of his taking charge, a fifteen per cent import duty imposed upon imported materials delayed paper delivery from three weeks to six months which had the potential of causing great problems for Butler and Tanner. With strawboards also incurring the same fifteen per cent duty but with imported books free of duty, it was feared that printers based in England would lose business as a direct result.[3] Turning his attention to those matters over which he did have control, he attempted to organise better the function of each department within the Company. He informed staff of the new organisational structure with a hand-drawn diagram published in the newsletter.[4]

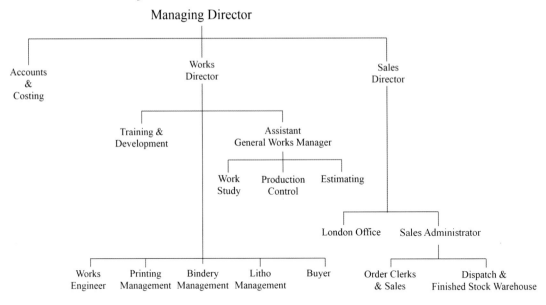

Staffing structure following a reorganisation of the works [4]

Those running the Company had long been concerned about lack of housing in the town. This, it was felt, was a significant factor in difficulties maintaining the necessary level of workforce, especially in attracting journeymen: essential in a seasonal business. Between 1966 and 1969 mortgages were taken out, by Butler and Tanner, on various plots on Critchill Park Estate. A few years earlier, in 1962, the Company had sponsored a competition for architects to design an estate of new houses on a five-acre site at Styles Hill, Frome.[5] It was hoped that by providing houses for rent within the town they would be able to attract and retain a greater number of trained workers.

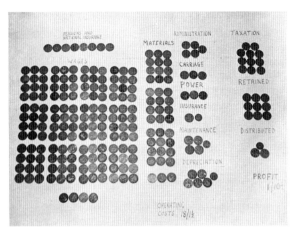

A visual representation of Butler and Tanner's expenditure

The high cost of wages had always presented a problem for those running the Company. Joseph Tanner once more used the medium of the newsletter to highlight to employees the significance of the demanding increase in wages. He created a visual representation of how the business's income was spent stating, 'You may like to work out for yourselves what a five per cent increase in wages would do to the distributable profits!'.6

At a board meeting in 1965 it was decided to purchase shares in St. Paul's Press in Malta for £10,000. The Maltese printer was to be reconstructed with Butler and Tanner taking over control of its management. St. Paul's Press's Managing Director later visited the Frome print works where it was agreed that a £60,000 debenture funded by the Bank of Malta would be taken out by Butler and Tanner. However, the deal ultimately proved unsuccessful as, in 1975, the shareholding in St. Paul's was written off and the Bank of Malta loan repaid.7

The Company hosted a wide variety of visitors over the years and were, at times, to find themselves in the centre of media reports. During the sixties some of their employees featured as subjects of a television programme. In 1968 the BBC visited Butler and Tanner: the BBC 2 television crew were to film the printing of a book entitled *Teach Yourself Sign Language*. To be broadcast in a ten-minute feature the programme was filmed in colour.8

Field Marshall Viscount Montgomery returned to Frome a decade after his first visit. In 1958 he had watched the printing of his published memoirs. This second trip to Butler and Tanner was undertaken to witness the binding of his book entitled *A Concise History of Warfare*: a 552-page volume of 80,000 copies.9 In 1969 Butler and Tanner sourced a new outlet for their business; that of Bible printing.

The BBC filming in Butler and Tanner's Lumitype department

The modern area housing the Lumitype department (had the photograph been in colour we would have been able to appreciate the 'pleasing visual effect' of its pale blue, yellow and white colour scheme

Securing a few contracts they were able to employ the Bristolian press in the manufacture of such volumes due to its capability of printing a densely inked page at a high speed because it incorporated a heat dryer.[10]

In 1970 Captain C.C. Flemming retired as Chairman and Joseph Russell Tanner replaced him. That year the Lumitype department moved into a new section adjacent to Litho Printing Down and Offset Camera Section to 'facilitate easier liaison on job details' for its fourteen workers. The clean and modern environment had been designed to be as dust-free as possible to ensure that the film wasn't damaged when being handled.[11] Having first purchased a Lumitype photo-composing machine in 1961 on a five-month trial, they had effectively embraced the technology over the years. The purchase of a two-colour offset press in 1966 was followed by a visit to Geneva and Cologne to investigate adapting 'idiot tape' for input to monotype, linotype and filmsetting. The firm applied to the Ministry of Technology for a grant to research mathematical typesetting in conjunction with Santype. Offset litho printing continued to grow and continual expansion in this area was vital to keep up with publishers' demands. Modernisation continued with the

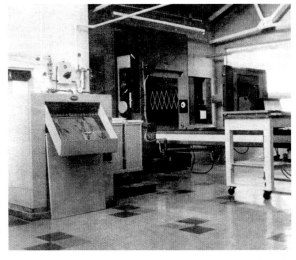

Part of the Camera Section indicating the delivery end of the PAKO processor, and lens and copyboard of the roll-film

installation of a new roll-film camera in the Offset Department in 1970. With offset printing established, the firm was manufacturing ninety plates a week with the majority of the film coming from Butler and Tanner's cameras. [12] In a factory, health and safety issues are always of importance and the newsletter represented a suitable forum in which to articulate various concerns. Workers were reminded of the need to use machine guards correctly and to ensure they wore no loose clothing which could potentially become trapped in machinery.

A Freccia 14 sewing machine

Additionally, in an interesting sign of the times, employees were reminded of the dangers posed by long hair in such a working environment, the newsletter stating, 'If you have long hair (girl or boy), wear a hat or tie it back'[13] It is presumed that they took heed of such common sense advice as the Company's continuing good safety record for the period resulted in their winning the British Safety Award for the third consecutive year in 1970.[14] With the proposed introduction of decimalisation in early 1971 all businesses within the country had to prepare for such a radical change. Its effects on Butler and Tanner were to be that banks would be closed for extra days to accommodate the new system resulting in paying wages for a week in advance for the first week in February 1971. The clocking-in system had to be adjusted so that an hour was calculated from quarters to tenths and fifths (6 and 12 minutes) and, finally, that pension contributions would be deducted for 50 weeks of the year instead of 52.[15] It was at this time that two new Freccia 14 sewing machines were purchased and installed, although delivery was later than expected due to Italian strikes affecting their manufacture. This increased the bindery's sewing capacity to include eighteen machines producing 1,400,000 sewn sections a week.[16] Additionally, a new Martini book jacketing machine installed in the bindery increased production to 3,000 jacketed books per hour. This automated the entire process from flat printed book jacket to the book being wrapped in its jacket.[17]

Four years previously, in 1968 Butler and Tanner, in conjunction with Elliott Automation Systems Ltd (later changed to G.E.C. Computers Ltd) had undertaken a research programme into computerised typesetting. As a result, by 1972, they decided to set up a Systems Typesetting Department in which to install a filmsetter and keyboards and it was

Machinery	Date purchased	Cost price
Bristolian Rotary m/c	1961	£63,000
DPE Rotary m/c	1967	£31,000
Mann NP56 Litho Perfector	1965	£20,800
Camco SC3P Folding m/c	1964	£6,600
2 x GSA Input Perforators	1968	£6,200
Lumitype Film Setting Equipment	1964 and 1971	£33,000 and £5,200
Sulby Bindmaster	1971	£4,700
Martini Jacketing m/c	1971	£6,335
Kodak Film Processor	1972	£3,600
Micro 16 Complete Computer and Teletype Units	1972	£14,500
Crabtree Mann SP72 Perfector Litho	1972	£55,000
Monophoto 600 Filmsetting Unit	1972	£32,500
Monotype 600 Keyboard	1972	£4,400
'Hiway' Keystor Keyboard and Verifier	1972	£2,950

Plant installed at Adderwell by 1972

hoped that the department would be in full operation by 1975 to 1976. Realising that it would require not only investment in the necessary hardware and software but also a considerable amount of staff training in order to grasp such pioneering concepts, directors took the sensible decision not to rush into this new mode of typesetting without careful research and forward planning.[18]

Problems caused by the 1972 national power cuts were alleviated by the firm's foresight in providing an alternative power supply to that of the national grid.[19] Additional night shifts were worked in order to ensure the generators were not overloaded during the day.

New boiler being delivered to Adderwell

These are remembered as something out of the ordinary with break times sometimes used to fetch fish and chip suppers and having to wait around in the middle of the night for lifts because the unfortunate driver had fallen asleep after a hard day's work.[20] The business had faced a few difficulties towards the end of the previous year with a drop in orders. This encouraged the London office into improving their effectiveness at the beginning of 1972 when the number of sales orders had 'increased considerably'.[21] With coal supplies disrupted and subsequent increases in the price of coal, the directors agreed to replace the old, inefficient boilers with automatic oil- or gas-fired plant at a total expenditure of £13,000.

The purchase of a more reliable film-setter was also proposed at a cost of £3,500 in view of the high level of spoiled film from the current machine. In addition, a reconditioned rounding and backing machine was to be bought for £10,700 as an alternative in case of breakdown but also to accommodate odd-sized books.[22] However, with disappointing sales, the rounder and backer was postponed together with the Monophoto-600.[23] Other factors were that an extension had to be built to accommodate the machinery and that appropriate wage rates for operating the Monophoto machinery had to be negotiated. Investment continued and in the autumn of 1972 a new Crabtree Sovereign litho

Crabtree Sovereign litho press being delivered

A new Crabtree Sovereign perfector up and running

press was purchased and delivered to the print works. Taking three weeks to set up, the Crabtree Sovereign perfector, the first of its size to be installed in the country was soon up and running at Butler and Tanner.[24]

Towards the latter part of 1972, building work began on an extension to provide additional accommodation for the bindery at Adderwell. It was duly completed and became fully operational by end of 1973.[25] Another notable event was the retirement of Mr Steele who had worked in the Company's London office for almost forty years. He had spent an initial three months in Frome to learn about Butler and Tanner and the printing trade before being based in the capital to obtain business from publishers. Following four years as a prisoner of war in Japan, he had resumed his position at the London office in 1946.

A valuation of machinery was undertaken in 1973 and this demonstrates the extent of

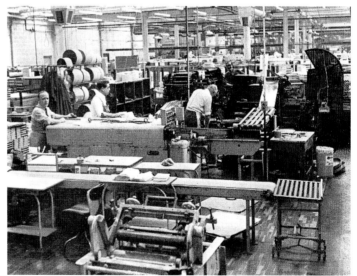

The cased book line in the extended bindery

expenditure in plant investment during that period of the Company's history. The valuation of the business totalled £1,073,352 with plant comprising £289,785.[26] This represents

90

substantial investment in equipment over the relatively short period of a decade.

In 1974 finances started to show signs of improvement, going from loss to a profit, but cash flow still remained a problem.[27] It was a difficult economic climate in which to conduct business but the report for the year ended 31st May, 1975 showed

Crabtree Sovereign Press c. 1975

that improvement from 1973/74's loss to profits of a record amount; assets increased from £206,000 to £409,000; short term indebtedness reduced by forty per cent and managed to contain the money tied

A female worker operating the Headrop Feeder c. 1975

up in stock and work in progress despite inflation.[28] The second half of 1975 proved especially difficult: the economic climate had forced competitors to make redundancies, put workers on short time and implement wage cuts but Butler and Tanner had managed to avoid these.[29] A lack of orders and having to take on orders at too low a price caused a decline in profitability whilst a slow turnaround in some areas of the manufacturing process caused delays and the subsequent loss of customers' goodwill.[30] The firm was in difficulties and a proposed merger with Andercroft/Santype, or closure, were considered as well as various cost savings:[31] amended pricing in line with inflation which was out of control; revision of wage structures; repayment of a high interest loan; early retirements to reduce staffing levels; adding half an hour to each working day; possible redundancies; reductions in overheads and improving the cash flow.[32]

Following the Equal Pay Act of 1970 and the Sexual Discrimination Act of 1975 women

could now demand the same wages as men for undertaking the same level of skilled work. In 1974, equal pay for women in the bindery of Butler and Tanner added one and a half per cent to the binding costs.[33]

In 1976 Frank Muir visited the print works to see his book being manufactured. Filmed by the BBC in the bindery at Butler and Tanner, his interview was broadcast on the regional news programme Points West. [34] Another visitor that year was former Prime Minister Harold Wilson who undertook a two-day visit to the factory in order to sign copies of his book *The Governance of Britain* published by

Frank Muir inspecting copies of his book, The Frank Muir Book, in the bindery at Butler and Tanner

Weidenfeld & Nicolson. This was no mean feat for he had been contracted by Book Club Associates to sign 5,000 copies of the 20,000 first print run. This was combined with participation in television, radio and press interviews over the same few days.[35]

In 1976 Butler and Tanner established a subsidiary publishing business in the form of a company called Springwood Books Ltd.[36] Its purpose was to handle the complete book manufacturing process, plus the sales and distribution, for customers not usually involved with their books (such as television companies, banks etc.).[37]

At the beginning of 1977 it was reported to staff that whilst the first half of the year had not been favourable, the second half had shown improvement with fuller order books than recently. However, it was acknowledged that competition was strong and some business had been lost to printers in India. For the majority of 1977 trading conditions remained difficult.[38]

Sir Harold Wilson made a return visit to Butler and Tanner where he proceeded to sign 10,000 of the 90,000 print run of his book *A Prime Minister on Prime Ministers* published by Weidenfeld & Nicolson. He managed the task over three days with staff placing the books before him and whipping them away in a production line fashion.[39] HTV filmed a

The Kolbus Flowline

programme in which they used the Butler and Tanner site for a street scene complete with a free-roaming tiger.[40] Direct exports for

customers were taken on by Butler and Tanner at this time. Until 1977 the only foreign customer they had worked for directly was dictionary publishers Langenscheidt of Munich. However, a new market evolved in the form of a Nigerian educational publisher resulting in orders for 350,000 books. Whilst it was a profitable venture, difficulties included: long distance communication via telex; full responsibility for editorial and proof reading duties; financial implications if the export administration was not in order; and finally, logistical and shipping issues.[41]

During 1978 the firm's cased binding capacity increased by twenty-five per cent due to installation of the first compact flowline in the country. This mechanised the binding process by incorporating processes into one – using a Perfecta Trimmer, Rounder and Backer linked to a Liner, Casing-in Station, Pressing unit and book stacker.[42]

The same year some Butler and Tanner workers found themselves in front of the cameras once again when the premises became a location for a health and safety film. Some employees were cast in roles which necessitated staging an accident and a subsequent visit to hospital.[43] Certainly not typical of the average working shift at the print works and probably the distraction was enjoyed by all involved. Other distractions undertaken during

The technology in use at Butler and Tanner for the photo-composition process, in 1980

the day-to-day running of the firm, typical of all factory environments included staff 'wind-ups'. Youngsters, generally apprentices, would be sent off on pointless errands from one side of the factory to the other. Such requests from older staff included 'fetching a left-handed screwdriver, a tub of elbow grease, a long weight, or in one case a K9P.'[44] Returning to their colleagues without the non-existent items no doubt caused much hilarity to fellow workers and embarrassment to the youngster. With the sale of the Selwood factory in 1979 the presence of the firm in the town's Trinity area was at an end.[45] In May of that year the letterpress department finally closed, representing the end of a very long era of printing tradition.

Unfortunately, the company of Butler and Tanner was struggling financially and had been for a few years. As a result they commissioned a report to try to discover the problems in order to find solutions. The report, by Ernst and Whinney set out to investigate the following matters: to give a full appraisal of the financial situation of Butler and Tanner; to discover the reasons for the current trading loss; to pinpoint problem areas; and to see what steps needed to be taken to place Butler and Tanner on a financially viable basis. By this period the business was described as that of 'typesetting, film-setting, printing and binding of books'.[46] The majority of the shares were still held by members of the Tanner family and the fifty-one year old Joseph Tanner was Chairman.

The firm's book manufacturing comprised several production processes: firstly, the composition or film-setting; secondly to the litho department for origination, plate-making and litho printing and; finally, binding. The manuscript would have been first keyed into the composing machine which automatically produced a paper tape upon which details relating to the book's character face, spacing etc. were recorded. The paper tape was then processed through a computer which transforms the punched tape into drive tape for the film-setting machine. This prints characters on photographic paper stored in specially designed cassettes which are developed to produce the proof copy of the book. Once proof read, the correct pages and illustrations are photographed and transparencies made of each page. For the next stage, plate making, the pages are sorted into collating order and inserted on a frame. A photographic/chemical process reproduces the transparencies onto aluminium or zinc plates. The plates are placed into the offset-litho printing presses and then printed onto paper. Once printed, the pages are collated, bound into folded sections, gathered together, trimmed and then bound into covers.[47]

Keyboard ▽   Filmsetter △

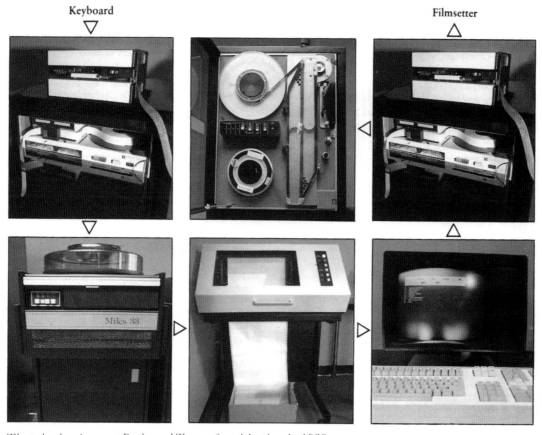

The technology in use at Butler and Tanner for origination, in 1980

A brochure, produced by Butler and Tanner in 1980 provides in-depth information into the technology used by them at the time. Photo-composition utilised: fourteen system input keyboards, operated on a shift basis, generated paper-tape which was processed by the central

The technology in use at Butler and Tanner for offset printing, in 1980

processing unit and stored on 80-megabyte disc for the filmsetter, or stored on magnetic tape. For filmsetting, a Lasercomp and two Monophoto 600 machines were in use.

Technology necessary for origination included: for the camera work cameras with computer-controlled exposure devices, a roll-film camera and automatic processors were in use. Any line drawings or diagrams were integrated into the made-up pages before conversion into film. Half-tone illustrations were converted into film separately rather than within the made-up pages.

Offset printing: the machine room housed eight presses, worked on shifts. For monochrome printing there were three Crabtree Sovereign perfectors and two Mann perfectors whilst for colour printing a Crabtree Sovereign two-colour, Mann two-colour and Roland Rekord two-colour presses were in use.

Having experienced financial difficulties towards the late seventies, succumbing to the country's economic recession which continued into the eighties, the firm was to head into the next decade facing similar problems.

Endnotes

[1] S.H. Steinberg, *Five Hundred Years of Printing*, New edition rev. by John Trevitt, The British Library and Oak Knoll Press, London, 1996, p. 220.
[2] *Ibid.*

3 *The Newsletter: Journal of the House of Butler & Tanner Ltd.*, No. 90 November–December 1964, Butler and Tanner, Frome, p. 4.

4 Staffing structure following a reorganisation of the works

5 *The Newsletter: Journal of the House of Butler & Tanner Ltd.*, No. 75 May–June 1962, Butler and Tanner, Frome, p. 9.

6 *The Newsletter: Journal of the House of Butler & Tanner Ltd.*, No. 102 November–December 1966, Butler and Tanner, Frome, pp. 4–5.

7 Joseph Tanner, 'A Selwood Scrapbook' [unpublished notes], Butler and Tanner Archive (DB5884/L2692), Frome, Somerset.

8 *The Newsletter: Journal of the House of Butler & Tanner Ltd.*, No. 108 January–April 1968, Butler and Tanner, Frome, p. 16.

9 'Monty to visit town in his role as author', *Somerset Standard*, 22nd March, 1968. Butler and Tanner Archive, Frome Museum, Frome, Somerset.

10 *The Newsletter: Journal of the House of Butler & Tanner Ltd.*, No. 112, July 1969, Butler and Tanner, Frome, p. 2.

11 *Newsletter: Journal of the House of Butler & Tanner Ltd.*, No. 117, 1970, Butler and Tanner, Frome, p. 1.

12 *Newsletter: Journal of the House of Butler & Tanner Ltd.*, No. 119, March 1970, Butler and Tanner, Frome, p. 1.

13 *Ibid.*, p. 2.

14 *Newsletter: Journal of the House of Butler & Tanner Ltd.*, No. 124, August 1970, Butler and Tanner, Frome, p. 1.

15 *Newsletter: Journal of the House of Butler & Tanner Ltd.*, No. 120, April 1970, Butler and Tanner, Frome, p. 4.

16 *Newsletter: Journal of the House of Butler & Tanner Ltd.*, No. 125, September 1970, Butler and Tanner, Frome, p. 1.

17 *Newsletter: Journal of the House of Butler & Tanner Ltd.*, No. 133, July–August 1971, Butler and Tanner, Frome, p. 2.

18 *Newsletter: Journal of the House of Butler and Tanner Ltd.*, No. 135 Winter 1971–2, pp. 5–8.

19 *Newsletter: Journal of the House of Butler and Tanner Ltd.*, No. 136, Spring 1972, p. 3.

20 Interview with former female employee of Butler and Tanner, 24th March, 2015.

21 *Ibid.*, p. 5.

22 *Newsletter: Journal of the House of Butler and Tanner Ltd.*, No. 136, Spring 1972, p. 5.

23 *Newsletter: Journal of the House of Butler and Tanner Ltd.*, No. 137, Summer 1972, p. 10.

24 *Newsletter: Journal of the House of Butler and Tanner Ltd.*, No. 138, Autumn 1972, p. 13.

25 *Newsletter: Journal of the House of Butler and Tanner Ltd.*, No. 142, Autumn 1973, p. 5.

26 Valuation, Colebrook, Evans and McKenzie 23rd July, 1973. Butler and Tanner Archive (DB5862), Frome Museum, Frome, Somerset.

27 *Newsletter: Journal of the House of Butler and Tanner Ltd.*, No. 146, Winter 1974–75 p. 4.

28 *Newsletter: Journal of the House of Butler and Tanner Ltd.*, No. 149, Autumn1975, p. 1.

29 *Newsletter: Journal of the House of Butler and Tanner Ltd.*, No. 150, Winter 1975–76 p. 5.

30 *Newsletter: Journal of the House of Butler and Tanner Ltd.*, No. 151, Spring/Summer 1976 p. 5.

31 Joseph Tanner, 'A Selwood Scrapbook', [unpublished notes], Butler and Tanner Archive (DB5884/L2692), Frome, Somerset.

32 *Ibid.*

33 *Ibid*

34 *Newsletter: Journal of the House of Butler and Tanner Ltd.*, No. 150, Winter 1975–76 p. 8.

35 *Newsletter: Journal of the House of Butler & Tanner Ltd.*, No. 152, Autumn 1976, Butler and Tanner, Frome, p. 1.

36 'Report, Butler and Tanner undertaken by Ernst & Whinney, August 1979, Butler and Tanner

Archive (DB4779/7696/3), Frome Museum, Frome, Somerset.

[37] *Newsletter: Journal of the House of Butler & Tanner Ltd.*, No. 153, Winter 1976–77, Butler and Tanner, Frome, pp. 2–3.

[38] *Newsletter: Journal of the House of Butler & Tanner Ltd.*, No. 154, July 1977, Butler and Tanner, Frome, pp. 2–3.

[39] *Newsletter: Journal of the House of Butler & Tanner Ltd.*, No. 155, 1977, Butler and Tanner, Frome, p. 1.

[40] *Newsletter: Journal of the House of Butler & Tanner Ltd.*, No. 155, 1977, Butler and Tanner, Frome, p. 4.

[41] *Newsletter: Journal of the House of Butler & Tanner Ltd.*, No. 155, 1977, Butler and Tanner, Frome, p. 6.

[42] *Newsletter: Journal of the House of Butler & Tanner Ltd.*, No. 156, 1978, Butler and Tanner, Frome, p. 1.

[43] *Newsletter: Journal of the House of Butler & Tanner Ltd.*, No. 157, 1978, Butler and Tanner, Frome, p. 7.

[44] Interview with Steve Burry, Christian Coates and Mike Barnsley, 15th March, 2015.

[45] H.W. Hallett, *The Newsletter: Journal of the House of Butler and Tanner Ltd*, September 1989, No. 1, Frome, Somerset, p. 19.

[46] 'Report, Butler and Tanner undertaken by Ernst & Whinney, August 1979, Butler and Tanner Archive (DB4779/7696/3), Frome Museum, Frome, Somerset.

[47] *Ibid*

EIGHT

Modern Times

The early 1980s were an extremely difficult period for the British book trade. With the country suffering from economic recession, around forty per cent of British printers went out of business during the period. Butler and Tanner made decisions in an endeavour to overcome the problems they knew they faced. Their strategy was to 'build on our strengths in human skills and ingenuity and aim for the high-quality, short-turn-round, quick-response market'.[1] When one particular Scottish-based printer became a casualty of the recession, Butler and Tanner purchased some of its equipment, specifically the first MBO large format folder, dismantling it and transporting it back to Frome for reassembly. Butler and Tanner, themselves, were also affected by the economy, having to make some staff redundant and make reductions in wages, difficult decisions taken to ensure the company's survival.[2]

Considering several options to help with the financial difficulties, a valuation of properties owned in Frome by Butler and Tanner was commissioned in 1981 with a view to selling them. It showed a large portfolio indicating the seriousness with which they had taken the issue of housing employees within the town. They owned: 1–10, 12 and 14 Easthill; 1, 2, 4 and 5 Caxton Road; 40–43 Adderwell Road; 41 Locks Hill; 37 and 39 Locks Hill; Canteen House, Caxton Road; and Canteen premises/Social club, Caxton Road, in Frome.[3]

By the mid-eighties things were improving financially for the business. Profitability improved and, by March of 1985 the six months' profit was greater than it had been for the whole of the previous year. By 1986 there came an end to the relief from corporation tax carried over from the loss-making years.[4] The same year, Butler and Tanner purchased the firm of Lawrence Allen, a commercial printing plant based in Weston-super-Mare. Comprising a bindery, pre-press department and a print works, the addition to the Group increased their output capacity. This was primarily to provide for the colour printing of book jackets and illustrations. The Company's finances had improved so much that over £1m profit was made for the first time.[5] Joseph Tanner and his colleagues soon realised that the way forward was to invest in the technology for colour printing and they purchased the largest machine available at the time, a Roland 800-7B.[6] The first book off the presses being, *Matchroom Snooker* (a title which, for obvious reasons, would clearly benefit from being printed in colour) for publisher Michael Joseph.[7]

Having been Managing Director since 1981, Mike Harman retired seven years later. Adrian Huett and Peter Maunder were appointed to the positions of joint Managing Directors to

BBC's Anneka Rice at Butler and Tanner

'improve synergy with Frome'.[8] Counteracting the recession had meant costly investment in plant and working capital, with a total of £7,500,000 being spent in an attempt to thwart the threat posed from European and Far Eastern competition. The purchase of that initial four-colour Roland 800-7B printer enabled them to increase their capacity greatly and they soon purchased three similar machines.[9] However, trading conditions continued to be difficult but a high profile contract resulted in the printing of Delia Smith's cookery books, 16 million copies of which were printed by Butler and Tanner during the 1980s and 1990s.[10] She was invited to the premises to inaugurate the third Roland press officially.

In 1989 Butler and Tanner won the award for Miller perfecting for monochrome printing.[11] The same year they played a major role in BBC 1's *Challenge Anneka* programme. The proposed remit was the compilation, paper making and manufacture of 10,000 copies of a joke book in a total of 36 hours, following a challenge from Friends of the Earth.

Employees rose to the task and the books were despatched with Anneka Rice for the launch in a London book shop. This episode proved an exciting undertaking of which the staff at Butler and Tanner could be proud.[12] However, the venture had its difficulties: members of the public were asked to ring the company with their jokes throughout the night which were to be set immediately by compositors. By two o'clock in the morning, a shortage of (suitable) material had necessitated the contacting of personal friends of Anneka Rice who worked as comedians, for appropriate jokes.[13]

The extent to which printing technology had changed over a century can be measured by looking at their range of plant in situ, by 1990. Bearing in mind that when the original Joe Tanner ran the business in the late nineteenth century, hand composition using hot metal and printing on letterpress machinery were utilised, the list of plant detailed below indicates the vast changes.

Plant at 1990
Filmsetting
14 offline input keyboards with disc conversion facilities
13 V.D.U. editing terminals
2 Monotype Lasercomps
3 Miles 33 front end composition systems

Pre-press
Flatbed scanner SF 222
2 Scanagraph SG 603
Misomex Colour Planner
Opticopy Imposition System

Printing
2 Four-colour Roland 800-V11B
2 Two-colour Roland Ultra V11
Two-colour Crabtree Sovereign
Two-colour Roland Rekord
5 Crabtree Sovereign Perfectors (monochrome printing)
Strachan and Henshaw Variquick (monochrome web printing)

Hardback Binding
6 MBO High speed Folders
2 Camco Knife Folders

26 Station Gathering Machines
14 Hand-fed Sewing Machines
6 Semi-automatic Sewing Machines
6 High-speed Fully Automatic Sewing Machines

Book Preparation/Casing In
2 Kolbus 40 Ratio/Compact binding lines supported by range of casemaking and blocking equipment

Paperback Binding
Muller Martini Monobloc with inline trimming and packing

Plant at Lawrence Allen/Knightstone Graphics
Colour Origination
Crosfield Magnascan 635 Laser Scanner
Autocompanica 650D Camera

Colour Proofing
Eurostandard Cromalin DA1 Nippon 2 colour proofing press

Printing
Six –colour Roland RSK 3B
Four-colour Komori Sprint
Four-colour Roland Rekord RV 3B
Two-colour Heidelberg Speedmaster 1022P two-colour Perfector
Heidelberg Sork (monochrome)

Binding
Brehmer Folding Machines
Brehmer Automatic nine-station Stitcher/Trimmer
Harris-Macey Multistation Stitching Line

Wrapping and Mailing
High-speed wrapping and mailing equipment[14]

Signs of another economic recession began in the late eighties and into the early nineties. Firstly, Lawrence Allen made financial losses, then the recession began to depress prices, a bad debt incurred by Phaidon and the cost of setting up the design section of £60,000 was written off. By 1991 the recession was having serious consequences and the Group's directors resolved to widen its customer base to include computer manuals and museum

Aerial view of the Adderwell works in 1994

catalogues to establish a market presence on the Continent, closing the repro department at Lawrence Allen and transferring it to their newest acquisition in nearby Radstock. In order to gain total control of production, in September 1991 Butler and Tanner acquired the total shareholding in Radstock Reproductions Ltd of nearby Midsomer Norton and a majority shareholding in Radstock Reproductions (Yeovil) Ltd. Equipped with a Dainippon Robotic Scanner and Sigmagraphic page make-up system, the four-colour origination company meant that Butler and Tanner would be able to fulfil another part of the manufacturing process inhouse.[15]

As in the recession of the early eighties, many of Butler and Tanner's competitors went out of business. There were mixed fortunes in the Butler and Tanner Group with the Frome works increasing profitability and Radstock Reproductions were profitable but the design section and film setting losing money and Lawrence Allen were losing 'control and money'.[16] The Tanner family's involvement in the firm ended with Joseph Tanner's retirement in 1994. In the same year the company newsletter was reinstated; printed for the first time in colour. Heralding the company's survival of yet another economic recession, its editorial tone was optimistic: 'It has been satisfying to see the Group come through a period of recession whilst continuing to grow and strengthen its position and reputation in the market. An on-going heavy capital investment programme coupled with

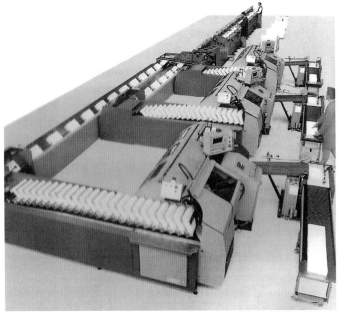

The Kolbus casing-in line

improved productivity and aggressive selling, has enabled us to compete head on with the major European book manufacturers.'[17] The same year two of their major competitors left the colour printing business with Butler and Tanner as the only remaining significant colour printer in Britain. The Group's turnover and profits rose, including those of Lawrence Allen.

Investment was the strategy by which the Board of Directors ran the company during the 1980s and 1990s. This, of course, was nothing new for a century earlier Joseph Tanner had adopted the very same policy. Having spent over £25 million in the decade spanning the late 1980s and early 1990s, further investment totalling £3,700,000 was planned for the mid-nineties. New colour printing presses were planned for instalment in both the Frome (in the guise of the fourth Roland) and Weston-super-Mare plants whilst an additional plate planner was added to aid the prepress. The bindery was enhanced by a new guillotine and a replacement line for the ribboning and jacketing processes was also to be installed.[18] A German sales office was set up in Munich to exploit further the European market.[19]

The Butler and Tanner Group acquired yet another asset in 1995. The purchase of Lloyds Register Printing Services located in West Sussex was made with the express aim of expanding the printing business to include that of company reports and accounts for city companies. Well equipped, the premises featured a range of mono/two-colour presses and a bindery comprising a Kolbus unsewn paperback line.[20] Upon completion of the purchase the firm was renamed Selwood Printing Ltd: a suitable link to the initial print works set up in Frome over a century earlier.

With business booming, Butler and Tanner were well placed to cope with the large print runs of bestsellers that the sales team had managed to secure. However, the one vital component for any printer is that of paper, and a shortage of this most basic of printing constituent presents a major concern. This problem was to be encountered yet again by Butler and Tanner in the mid-nineties. With an increase in demand and the paper mills not responding to this demand, the ability to acquire paper both readily and cost effectively was proving difficult for them. With serious shortages the cost of paper pulp rose from £200 per tonne to £450 per tonne from the beginning of 1994 to the autumn of that year and it was expected to reach £650 per tonne before the end of the year. Staff members were urged, therefore, to be especially careful to avoid wastage. [21]

Yet again, five years after its initial encounter with the BBC's production staff, the printers rose to another challenge involving Anneka Rice. This time the charity, 'Breakthrough Charity for Breast Cancer' had tasked Anneka with the production of a recipe book in 48 hours. The magnificent team at Butler and Tanner made it happen just as they had previously with everything from the pre-press to the final printed copies being handled by the staff within the Group.[22]

Financially, 1994 had proven to be a successful year for the Group with a turnover of £30 million and a pre-tax profit of £1,503,000.[23] Having gained success with the opening of a European office, the Group decided to grow further geographically and, in 1995 opened an office in New York in order to take advantage of the US market.[24] Things remained positive throughout the rest of the nineties. The company continued to win awards for the quality of their work: the 1995 Printer of the Year sponsored by Midland Bank and BPIF[25] and the 1996 Winner of the *Printing World*'s: The Dainippon Screen Award for Fine Art Printing; and the 1996 Winner of *PrintWeek*'s UK Book Printer of the Year.[26]

Equally satisfying for them was the production of the fastest selling book ever produced by the company; Delia Smith's *Winter Collection* which had sold 1,750,000 copies before Christmas of 1995.[27] She also visited Butler and Tanner, sending them a letter to thank

Norma Major visiting Butler and Tanner to see her book being printed

them for their hospitality.[28] Yet another guest was Norma Major (the Prime Minister, John Major's wife) who posed for photographs beside copies of her book, *Chequers*, printed by Butler and Tanner. They presented her with a framed sheet of gold foil from the production line.[29] Due to commercial optimism during this period, it was decided to undertake major building extension work to the Bindery and Despatch areas at Adderwell.

One particularly dreadful incident, however, was the destruction of one section of the print works due to a fire. Having had a couple of fires at the old Selwood premises at the beginning of the twentieth century, fire insurance had been a necessity and fire safety precautions good practice. As a result there had been no such problems for a long period until 1996 when a fire at the company's Marston factory, caused by a faulty thermostat on the adhesive tank, caused a great deal of damage. With ruined machinery and the premises needing extensive repair, employees worked tirelessly to sort out as much as possible whilst contractors cleaned smoke-damaged machinery and re-roofed the building.[30] In order to continue running this part of the business until the repairs could be completed,

Michael Palin inspecting printed sheets at Butler and Tanner

Aerial photo of the Adderwell works taken in 1997

staff were sent to use the equipment at Burgess Hill. For approximately four months the Frome staff boarded on a weekly basis in West Sussex so as to be able to continue to work for Butler and Tanner. They spent Monday to Thursday working night shifts so as not to interrupt the work already being undertaken at the West Sussex premises. [31]

The Group continued to attract high profile accounts and they received a letter from Michael Palin thanking them for quality of work on his *Full Circle* book.[32] He had earlier paid a visit to the print works to see his book being manufactured.[33] Similarly, Martyn Lewis visited to witness the printing of his own book during 1997. The same year Butler and Tanner won 'Book Printer of the Year' for second consecutive year.[34]

Martyn Lewis signing copies of his book at Butler and Tanner

In 1998 the print works successfully manufactured its largest single order: *The Illustrated Encyclopaedia of Healing Remedies*, published by Element Books. The subject matter of the 496-page volume was of healing common ailments using alternative therapies and remedies. With an initial print run of 182,000 copies the supporting statistics of its manufacture are impressive: utilising 1,500 miles worth of paper the final bound books covered 550 pallets and filled the equivalent of 20 40-ft lorries. With 900 hours of machining time and just under 100 hours to bind, the manufacture of these colour-printed books was a significant achievement.[35] This period was a positive one for the company as Adrian Huett, joint Managing Director at the time, told the workers, 'good orders secured and an over-valued pound weakening for the first time in over two years, there is a sign of more healthy times ahead.'[36] Butler and Tanner Incorporated in New York now made up approximately twenty-five per cent of the Company's business.[37] This grew to represent an important branch of the company with gross sales from that market reaching $10m by 2005. One particularly successful contract for the American market was the printing of a *Soprano's Cook Book* which necessitated a reprint every week. Four of the six presses were kept busy for forty hours a week producing 100,000 copies of the book to be subsequently air-freighted to the U.S. This feat was maintained from October to December in order to keep up with demand.[38] A new pre-press area was created at Selwood Printing to accommodate the delivery of an Infoprint 4000 machine which was installed by IBM engineers.[39] The digital press was delivered and installed in 1998.[40]

Richard Noble's visit to Butler and Tanner

The purpose-built design studio

The positive year continued with Butler and Tanner winning not only 'Book Printer of the Year' but also the prestigious overall 'Printer of the Year'. The latter being for a publication entitled Power of the Poster published by V & A Publications. They also opened an office in Paris in 1998.[41] Richard Noble visited the Frome premises to witness his publication *Thrust*, published by Transworld, being printed.[42] Investment this year included the construction of a purpose-built studio to accommodate their designers. Built at a cost of £25,000, the studio was situated in the grounds of the main Butler and Tanner factory.[43]

The following year digital printing was introduced to Butler and Tanner, at Selwood Printing, in the form of two IBM Infocolor 100 Web machines and two Mono Infoprint 4000 machines. Exports for the previous year, it was reported in March 1999, had amounted to 5,300,000 books.[44] They also won *Print Week*'s 'Book Printer of the Year' for the third consecutive year[45] along with *Printing World*'s 'UK Book Printer of the Year'.[46]

One visitor to the Frome works was a young, unknown chef; a lad by the name of Jamie Oliver. He came to the print works to see his book *Naked Chef* being manufactured. Just a few years later he returned as an extremely well-known high profile television celebrity. [47]

Jamie Oliver visiting Butler and Tanner to see his book being printed

The new millennium heralded huge investment in colour printing technology: a new digital colour press was installed at Selwood Printing to strengthen the short print-run capacity: a Xerox Docucolor 2060 which could print 60 pages per minute and was one of the fastest sheet-fed digital colour presses available.[48]

Additionally, the firm installed new colour KBA presses the first three being five-colour and the rest six-colour which signified a major investment.[49] However,

The KBA machine room

to be cost-effective, the presses would have to support enough work. The book printing trade is particularly seasonal in nature with the busiest three months in the summer period (July to September). Thus, presses need to be kept at full capacity all year round and it was hard to obtain sufficient sales. As had been experienced throughout industry since the

Industrial Revolution, mechanisation inevitably meant job losses by 'demanning' with machine assistants losing their jobs. Applying 'full cost recovery' staff were made redundant and the remaining staff had to work harder.[50]

In 1999 a decision had been made to widen the customer base. Efforts were made to gain contracts for commercial printing to provide additional business alongside that of book printing. By 2001 such contracts had duly been won by the sales team including: volume cataloguing work for Barbour, Contact and Riba; and annual reports and accounts for companies

Examples of posters for commercial printing by Butler and Tanner

including Shell and Associated British Ports.[51] Commercial printing was nothing new to the firm and had formed the core of its business in its earliest days of the nineteenth century.

The death of Her Majesty Queen Elizabeth the Queen Mother in the spring of 2002 prompted efforts on behalf of Butler and Tanner's staff reminiscent of those required to rise to Anneka Rice's

Queen Mother's Century being printed at Butler and Tanner

previous challenges. Over the Easter weekend, employees came into work to man the presses for the printing of three titles dedicated to a celebration of the life of the Queen Mother. [52] The main body of the volumes had already been printed in preparation for such an event and just the first and last sections had to be printed. On the afternoon of Easter Saturday, directors received a telephone call to explain that due to Her Majesty's death the book required printing immediately. A strategy meeting was called for Saturday evening and printing staff called in for the Sunday. The books were folded and sewn on Easter Monday with the binding undertaken that evening. The completed books were despatched

from the Adderwell works on Tuesday. As usual, Butler and Tanner workers had risen to the task and worked tirelessly to produce the

KBA Rapida

volumes in an exceptionally short time frame.[53]

That same year Butler and Tanner took delivery of an enormous press, the KBA Rapida 162a. Seven lorries were required to haul the machinery which necessitated some very careful offloading. Once deposited at the print works it then took four weeks to build.[54] Highlights of 2003 included a visit from, the now well-known, Jamie Oliver together with his family. They had travelled to Frome in order to celebrate the publication of his latest cookery book, *Jamie's Kitchen*, printed by Butler and Tanner.[55] That year Peter Maunder became non-executive Chairman of Butler and Tanner whilst Adrian Huett became its sole Managing Director having previously shared the role with Maunder.[56] In 2003 they won the 'Book Printer of the Year' award for the sixth time in seven years. The following year they also won *PrintWeek*'s 'Brochure Printer of the Year' proving that diversification from the core business did not mean sacrificing standards[57] as well as winning *Printing World*'s 'Digital Printer of the Year'.[58]

New business gained during this period included the printing of four million copies of the cover for the Ikea catalogue[59] and 631,000 copies of the 'Sustainable Development Report'.[60] Additional contracts were awarded as a result of the firm gaining ISO 14001 status, particularly one for the commercial printing contract to produce the Vodafone Report and Accounts and another for 2.2 million copies of the 'Shell Annual Report'. Additionally, 'Marks and Spencer's Report and Accounts', 'British Gas Annual Report and Accounts' and the 'Annual Report and Accounts for R.B.S' were all printed at Butler and Tanner during that period. Printing these corporate documents may have influenced those in charge for during that year the Butler and Tanner Group initiated a new corporate identity to provide a unity between all the disparate entities within the group. [61] Adding another area for diversification, Butler and Tanner launched a new business that they named 'Heritage in Print', selling personalised calendars via an e-commerce website using images sourced from a variety of collections.[62]

They also took on their largest project to date: a 60-volume tome. The *Oxford Dictionary of National Biography,* containing 50,000 biographies was compiled by a total of 10,000 specialists from around the world. Twelve years in its compilation, it encompassed sixty million words, cost £7,500 per set and each set weighed twenty stone.[63] Printing of such a large contract would have required great commitment.

By this period the British printing industry faced strong competition from emerging economies, in particular, the Far East. No-one at this time realised how great the threat from China would ultimately prove to be. Prices soon plummeted as whole swathes of printing work moved to Asia. All European printers were chasing an ever decreasing market for their services. This marked the end of the 'glory days' and was the start of the decline of Butler and Tanner.[64] The company was soon to enter the final stages of its existence. The next few years were to prove the most volatile in its history, ultimately leading to the collapse of what had once been an illustrious printing company.

Endnotes

[1] Joe Tanner, *The Newsletter: Journal of the House of Butler and Tanner Ltd*, September 1989, No. 1, Frome, Somerset, p. 1.

[2] H.W. Hallett, *The Newsletter: Journal of the House of Butler and Tanner Ltd*, September 1989, No. 1, Frome, Somerset, p. 19.

[3] Valuation of Residential Properties situated in Frome and owned by Butler and Tanner, 9th July, 1981, Butler and Tanner Archive (DB4779/D7696/2), Frome Museum, Frome, Somerset.

[4] Joseph Tanner, 'A Selwood Scrapbook', [unpublished notes], Butler and Tanner Archive (DB5884/L2692), Frome, Somerset.

[5] *Ibid.*

[6] *Ibid.*, p. 85.

[7] *The Butler and Tanner Group Newsletter*, Issue No. 13, February 1998, p. 1.

[8] Joseph Tanner, 'A Selwood Scrapbook', [unpublished notes], Butler and Tanner Archive (DB5884/L2692), Frome, Somerset.

[9] *The Newsletter: Journal of the House of Butler and Tanner Ltd*, September 1989, No. 1, p. 2.

[10] 'A short history of Butler and Tanner', article in Butler and Tanner Archive (D8652 and DB5706), Frome Museum, Frome. Somerset.

[11] *The Newsletter: Journal of the House of Butler and Tanner Ltd*, December 1989, No. 2, p. 31.

[12] *The Newsletter: Journal of the House of Butler and Tanner Ltd*, December 1989, No. 2, pp. 15–16.

[13] Joseph Tanner, 'A Selwood Scrapbook' [unpublished notes], Butler and Tanner Archive (DB5884/L2692), Frome, Somerset.

[14] Butler and Tanner Complete Works, Butler and Tanner, Frome, Somerset, 1990, pp.46–48.

[15] *The Newsletter: Journal of the House of Butler and Tanner Ltd*, August 1991, No. 6, p. 4.

[16] Joseph Tanner, 'A Selwood Scrapbook', [unpublished notes], Butler and Tanner Archive (DB5884/L2692), Frome, Somerset.

[17] *The Butler and Tanner Group Newsletter*, Issue No. 1, February 1994, p. 1.

[18] *The Butler and Tanner Group Newsletter*, Issue No. 2, June 1994, pp. 2–3.

[19] *The Butler and Tanner Group Newsletter*, Issue No. 1, February 1994, p. 6.

[20] *The Butler and Tanner Group Newsletter*, Issue No. 3, October 1994, p. 1.

[21] *The Butler and Tanner Group Newsletter*, Issue No. 3, October 1994, p. 2.

[22] *Ibid.*, p. 3.

[23] *The Butler and Tanner Group Newsletter*, Issue No. 4, February 1995, p. 4.

24 *The Butler and Tanner Group Newsletter*, Issue No. 6, October 1995, p. 4.

25 *The Butler and Tanner Group Newsletter*, Issue No. 7, February 1996, p. 2.

26 *The Butler and Tanner Group Newsletter*, Issue No. 10, February 1997, p. 5.

27 *The Butler and Tanner Group Newsletter*, Issue No. 7, February 1996, p. 2.

28 Letter [framed] from Delia Smith to Butler and Tanner, 13th February, 1996. Butler and Tanner Archive, Frome Museum, Frome, Somerset.

29 Letter [framed] from Norma Major to Butler and Tanner, 26th November, 1996. Butler and Tanner Archive, Frome Museum, Frome, Somerset.

30 *The Butler and Tanner Group Newsletter*, Issue No. 9, October 1996, p. 8.

31 Interview with Steve Burry, 13th March, 2015.

32 Letter [framed] from Michael Palin to Butler and Tanner, 25th July, 1997. Butler and Tanner Archive, Frome Museum, Frome, Somerset.

33 *The Butler and Tanner Group Newsletter*, Issue No. 12, October 1997 p. 2.

34 *The Butler and Tanner Group Newsletter*, Issue No. 13, February 1998, p. 5.

35 *The Butler and Tanner Group Newsletter*, Issue 14, June 1998, pp. 1–2.

36 *Ibid.*

37 *The Butler and Tanner Group Newsletter*, Issue 14, June 1998, p. 3.

38 Interview with Steve Burry, 13th March, 2015.

39 *The Butler and Tanner Group Newsletter*, Issue 14, June 1998, p. 3.

40 *The Butler and Tanner Group Newsletter*, Issue No. 13, February 1998, p. 15.

41 *The Butler and Tanner Group Newsletter*, Issue 15, October 1998, p. 5.

42 *Ibid.*, p. 6.

43 *The Butler and Tanner Group Newsletter,* Issue 15, October 1998, p. 11.

44 *The Butler and Tanner Group Newsletter*, Issue 16, March 1999, pp.1–3.

45 *Ibid.*, p. 5.

46 *The Butler and Tanner Group Newsletter*, Issue No. 18, October 1999, p. 1.

47 *The Butler and Tanner Group Newsletter*, Issue No. 17, June 1999, p. 6.

48 *The Butler and Tanner Group Newsletter*, Issue No. 22, February 2001, p. 27.

49 *Ibid.*, pp. 2–3.

50 Interview with former printer, Butler and Tanner, 18th February, 2015.

51 *The Butler and Tanner Group Newsletter*, Issue No. 25, February 2002, p. 8.

52 *The Butler and Tanner Group Newsletter*, Issue No. 26, June 2002, pp. 2–3.

53 Interview with Steve Burry, 13th March, 2015.

54 *The Butler and Tanner Group Newsletter*, Issue No. 27, October 2002, p. 13.

55 *Ibid.*, pp. 2–3.

56 'Young guns in charge at B&T', *Printing World*, 3rd July, 2003.

57 *The Butler and Tanner Group Newsletter*, Issue No. 31, February 2004, p. 6.

58 *The Butler and Tanner Group Newsletter*, Issue No. 33, October 2004, p. 12.

59 *The Butler and Tanner Group Newsletter*, Issue No. 28, February 2003, p. 5.

60 *The Butler and Tanner Group Newsletter*, Issue No. 29, June 2003, p. 2.

61 *The Butler and Tanner Group Newsletter*, Issue No. 32, June 2004, pp. 2–3.

62 *The Butler and Tanner Group Newsletter*, Issue No. 33, October 2004, p.2.

63 'A short history of Butler and Tanner', article in Butler and Tanner Archive (D8652 and DB5706), Frome Museum, Frome. Somerset.

64 Interview with Steve Burry, 13th March, 2015.

NINE

Butler, Tanner and Dennis

The final few years in the company's history were particularly turbulent. Having survived two world wars, several periods of economic depression, the demise of proprietors, periods of workers' unrest and strike action, a transfer of premises and countless day-to-day difficulties, the firm was to experience insurmountable problems in the latter part of its existence.

In 2006 Joseph Russell Tanner died.[1] Having outlived his first wife, Fenella, by twenty five years,[2] his second marriage, to Geraldine Akerman took place in 1993. He was the last member of the Tanner family to have an association with the company. It is evident from speaking to some of his former colleagues that Joseph had been universally well liked. One obituary defined his working relationships thus: 'He knew everyone in the firm by sight and voice and name, and their spouses and most of their children. He took a keen and wholly unpatronising interest in everything they did, their work and what they did outside. To them he was just 'Mr Joe'.'[3] In addition, he was greatly respected for his knowledge of the printing trade and as a businessman: 'For 30 years he was in charge of this progress; in a time of rapid and radical change, he never put a foot wrong, and it was his skill, both technical and in what he would have been the last to call 'management', that made the revolution peaceful as well as successful.'[4]

At the end of 2005, a few months before Joseph Tanner died, the premises at Adderwell were sold in order to release capital for the pension fund. Purchased by London and County property developers, a deal was negotiated that involved leasing back the works whilst the firm continued to function as it had previously at the same site within the same buildings. The following year further refinancing was secured by utilising the assets of the firm's pension scheme and negotiating a deferral of payments. Unfortunately, the premises were now even more costly and too large for the company to operate in a market shrinking by competition from overseas. At this juncture both Pete Maunder and Adrian Huett left the company. However, Butler and Tanner's pension deficit of around £10 million was the explanation given for the halting of a proposed takeover by Media & Print Investments. The group subsequently purchased the firm out of administration, in August 2007, immediately following a 'pre-pack' agreement.

Employees must have felt very unsettled whilst this was taking place but, nevertheless, conducted their everyday business in their usual manner. Despite the firm's troubles, workers continued to manufacture high-quality books and, again, won another printing award in the same year. The autumn of 2007 was particularly busy and signs for early 2008 looked positive. Other companies in the same sector owned by the parent company, including the Friary Press were relocated to the Adderwell premises to consolidate the work to account for quieter periods. However, the management had still not been able to tackle the lack of orders for colour printing and the seasonality that had always been an issue in the market. A difficult financial situation was being faced, by the new owner Mike Dolan, with a predicted massive loss in turnover and a solution had to be found in order to save the business. A viable solution proved impossible, however and in April 2008, all 287 staff members were made redundant due to an ensuing dispute. According to the Union, he had tried to 'impose cuts to pay and conditions on staff at Butler and Tanner as well as making demands on working time, holidays and shift patterns which went well below print industry standards.'[5] The Unite chapel found the terms unacceptable, which led to a bitter and lawful dispute at its Frome factory in Somerset'. Mike Dolan subsequently placed the firm into voluntary liquidation. Feelings were running high and after finding themselves locked out of the premises with the gates chained and guarded by security guards, workers took to the streets in a mass demonstration to protest at the treatment they had endured at the new owners' hands.[6]

By 2013 Mike Dolan and Ben Crozier of MPI had been disqualified as directors for eight years. The Insolvency Service issued a statement explaining the decision of the court, 'MPI had breached its factoring agreement by raising two false invoices totalling £440,461 and

Formula One driver, Jenson Button, with his book printed by Butler and Tanner

obtaining payment on them. In addition, assets subject to fixed charges were sold and the company failed to pay the proceeds to the charge holder, which suffered a loss estimated at £545,378. The court also found that the group companies made payments to their own management companies at a time when creditors were not being paid.'[7] David Brooks, a chief examiner for the Insolvency Service, said: 'Actions taken with company assets have to be carried out with regard to creditors and others with interests in those assets… …Transactions at the latter stages of a company's existence, when it is insolvent, need to be carried out with care with a view to the directors' duties to all creditors and the company, not just to themselves.'

With the business closed and all the plant having been put up for sale at auction, at the eleventh hour a benefactor in the shape of Felix Dennis provided funds to acquire the assets. Renamed Butler, Tanner and Dennis, the firm reopened on 1st August 2008 with Kevin Sarney taking on the role of Managing Director. The reason for Felix Dennis's involvement was that, having already had four of his poetry books printed by Butler and Tanner and having been pleased with the quality, when his latest book of poetry required printing he contacted the firm. However, at this point the enquiry was met with the apologetic response that Butler and Tanner would no longer be able to print his book

Felix Dennis who took over the firm in 2008

since they were in administration. Apparently, infuriated Felix condemned the situation and ordered the purchase of the stricken printer. With a passionate phone call to his Finance Director, Ian Leggett, Dennis said 'We must save this business and retain the ability in the UK to produce and bind big colour books'[8] and saved a high quality British printing company and its skilled workforce. Dennis was enamoured with the Butler and Tanner story and set up a trust fund to help alleviate what was described as the 'pain of the Dolan debacle'.[9] This was not a business decision but an emotive one by the book loving Dennis. Therefore, he bought the firm and his book, *Homeless in my Heart*, followed by several others, was duly printed.[10] Felix Dennis had been a pioneer in magazine publishing since the 1960s, setting up his publishing company, Dennis Publishing in the mid-1970s. He had taken the company to success both in Britain and the United States.

He began writing poetry in 2001 and his published poetry was followed by a tour to perform his works adding to his portfolio with non-fiction works.

Book printing continued at the Frome plant and one high profile

Heidelberg Press XL162 installed in 2011

account included the printing, in 2009, of a book featuring Formula One racing driver, Jenson Button. A native of the area, he made a visit to nearby Bath where he was photographed with the book My Championship Year together with a member of Butler and Tanner's staff who had also attended the same Frome school as Jenson.

In an attempt to even out the production workloads in a seasonal trade, a contract was sought and won for the printing of maps. In September 2010, the company of Butler, Tanner and Dennis was awarded a five-year contract to print Ordnance Survey maps. As highly experienced printers with an impressive array of printing technology at their disposal they were well placed to take on the role. Once the techniques involved in the map folding and casing had been understood production of the maps could commence. Initially, the project involved just the finishing of the smaller maps whilst the original Ordnance Survey factory continued to print the maps and finish off those larger ones. However, after a few weeks production moved wholesale to Butler, Tanner and Dennis so that by the end of the following year the firm had printed almost two million maps.[11] The map printing division, though owned by the parent company Butler, Tanner and Dennis Holdings, was established as a separate limited company entitled Butler, Tanner and Dennis Maps Ltd,

to protect the Ordnance Survey contract. A fortuitous move as, four years later, when Butler, Tanner and Dennis closed at least the map division could be salvaged and continues to provide employment for over twenty former employees. Relocating from the Adderwell site the new

Last few days of Butler, Tanner and Dennis

Printing of Butler and Tanner's final book

company now entitled Dennis Maps Ltd, remains in Frome with Managing Director, Steve Burry running the business.[12]

The following year, a decision was made to invest in a new press, a Heidelberg Speedmaster XL162; the first such in the country. With a running speed of 15,000 sheets per hour it certainly had a large capacity and an extremely quick make-ready capability: the problem would be maintaining the amount of work to make it a worthwhile investment.

Among various strategies to ensure the firm's survival, the Board of Butler, Tanner and Dennis discussed a merger with Berforts Information Press Group (a long-established printer with facilities in Hastings, Stevenage and Eynsham). However, there were various areas of disagreement with one of the most significant issues being the location of the operation. When it was suggested that the business needed to leave Frome the merger did not happen. Managing director, Kevin Sarney left the firm at this juncture and Gerald White was appointed Chief Executive Officer.

The Adderwell site owners put in planning permission for it to be redeveloped for residential and commercial purposes but a year's extension to the lease was negotiated with the owners. The extension was to last a year running from September to September 2014. However, the company subsequently went into administration in May 2014. The reasons given for the company's final collapse included: 'uncertainties over its existing site, on-going losses and prevailing market conditions'.[13] With the planned redevelopment of the site following the expiration of the lease a search for alternative premises ensued but no suitable site was identified.

Felix Dennis issued the following statement: 'It is with a heavy heart that I have supported the Board's decision to place Butler Tanner & Dennis Ltd into administration. Since my involvement in 2008, I have invested a great deal of time, money and energy to help create a sustainable book printing business in Frome. However site issues and challenging market conditions have ultimately forced our hand. It is an extremely sad day for British book printing to lose this fantastic accumulation of talent and heritage. I am indebted to past and present staff at Frome and to customers and suppliers for all their support, hard work and dedication.'[14]

With the business closed, Felix Dennis died in June of that year, undoubtedly much to the sadness of all former Butler, Tanner and Dennis employees. His cash injection, in excess of £12m, had been vital in keeping the firm in business towards the end of his life and that of the company. Felix Dennis kept the business going throughout the administration and supported the staff by guaranteeing generous payments on their redundancies. The final days of printing at the Adderwell works were captured for posterity and the stages of the final book to be printed documented in the illustrations below.

A company is nothing without its employees and the firm of Butler and Tanner has been rewarded with some very loyal workers over its long and illustrious history. As has been mentioned previously, many employees spent their entire working lives with the firm with fifty years of service not being at all unusual. Staff records were meticulously kept and all the index cards now reside in the company's archive. These provide a fascinating insight into, arguably, the firm's most vital component, its human resources. Therefore, rather than ending the story on a sombre note, the memory of the firm should act as a tribute to those people who made it possible; aside from the Tanner family themselves: the workers. With the records spanning well over a century they reveal some interesting historical reasons for the departure of employees. In some instances it was Butler and Tanner themselves who initiated the departure of its workers: some had to be laid off due to shortage of work; some were given their notice because their work was 'not up to standard' or for 'playing about'; others were simply 'no good' or sacked for such reasons as 'refusal to work', 'not a member of the union', 'continuously playing about', 'for faulty work', 'for defective eyesight', 'inattention to work' or 'slackness of work'. Some were laid off when the Adderwell works was requisitioned and others when the purchase of new machinery inevitably meant that the level of labour required for a process to be undertaken would be considerably reduced. One employee was 'sent off at a moment's notice for reading novels whilst running his machine'; one was sacked for 'gross insubordination' whilst another 'absconded'. One young girl lost her job when 'owing to illness fell down Binding Room stairs, not safe to be amongst machinery' whilst another because she was 'objected to by other employees, they consider her an unsuitable work mate'. One was sacked for threatening and swearing at a colleague whilst another (a thirteen year old lad) was sacked for 'taking money from other men's coats in the Foundry'.

The reasons for workers leaving the employ of Butler and Tanner of their own accord were varied: retirement, death, joining H.M. Forces (this was, predictably, a very common reason during the First and Second World Wars as well as during the post-war period when National Service had been introduced) or Land Army or for munitions work; going abroad; youngsters who were too young to stay in the area when their parents moved away; some simply gave their notice citing reasons such as 'not liking the work'. By far the most common reason for female employees leaving the company was to get married. Some young girls were obliged to leave for family reasons such as 'to keep house owing to father's illness' or 'to look after invalid mother until her death' or 'mother ill had to stay home'. One fourteen year old 'ran away'. One 'left to go to hospital where he died' whilst another, tragically 'left his work and was found drowned at Elm'.[15]

A very large number of workers spent their entire working lives with the firm. Upon retirement they were awarded gifts from the company in gratitude for their work over the years. It is recalled that some staff members such as Mr Pobjoy and Mr Henley managed sixty years of service for which they each received a gold watch. The retirees were allowed to choose their own present from shops in the town; for example Sally Bowden chose a music centre and her brother chose a watch, whilst Jean Hicks opted for a portable television.[16] Others preferred a cheque and the newsletters are full of presentations for a multitude of retiring workers.

Not only a place of employment for many people in the town of Frome, Butler and Tanner continued to provide a social outlet in many forms: the sports and social club (named the Caxton Club) provided premises in which staff could meet up in a relaxing environment for a (subsidised) drink or two, play a game of snooker, table skittles or darts or watch television. The firm had a prize-winning football team (it triumphed in the National Print Cup in the 1998/99 season) and table tennis team (won North-east Somerset Table Tennis League Division 3 Championship), organised parties for retired employees, held cricket tournaments, participated in charity bingo events, hosted children's Christmas parties, held fishing matches and countless other social opportunities. Green-fingered employees achieved 'Very Highly Commended' in the Frome in Bloom competition in 1998. There is a saying 'there's many a match made in heaven' but it appears that Butler and Tanner could also be a contender for the accolade having facilitated the coupling of many employees over the decades. The firm's newsletter reported employees' weddings with a very large number of them comprising Butler and Tanner employees as both bridegroom and bride.

Once the administrators had been called in for the final time, the premises had to be cleared and the large equipment moved out of the building. Extracting the huge

Heavy lifting gear needed to remove the heavy plant from the Adderwell works

machinery would, inevitably prove as difficult a logistical task as it had been for their initial installation.

Premises which had housed the print works since the beginning of the twentieth century were to stand empty little over a hundred years later. There is an irony in the fact that, with the granting of planning permission for the site to be used for the building of homes for local people the solution to the housing problem that blighted the company for so long would finally be found. Sadly, there are now no large scale employers within the town to provide the work to attract them here. It has been suggested to the author by a former Butler and Tanner printer that those new streets forming the residential area to arise from the Adderwell site should be appropriately named. Perhaps the legacy will live on in a Tanner Avenue, Sovereign Street, Crabtree Close, Roland Road, Bristolian Boulevard, or some such tribute to such an important part of the town's history.

With the closure of Butler, Tanner and Dennis in 2014, the employees not only lost their employment but also a social community which had been sustained for well over a hundred years. The Tanner family, and Felix Dennis, have cause to be proud of the part they played in the town; not only providing a livelihood for hundreds of townsfolk but providing a whole way of life for many. Additionally, all those individuals who became members of the Butler and Tanner 'family' can take pride in their contribution for they truly did make an impression on Frome's printing past.

Final before and after photographs of the interior of the Adderwell premises

Endnotes

[1] Obituary, *Somerset Standard*, Frome, Somerset. 27th April, 2006.

[2] Obituary, *The Times*, London. 4th May, 2006.

[3] Obituary, *The Independent*, 29th April, 2006.

[4] Obituary, *The Independent*, 29th April, 2006.

[5] 'Former print boss disqualified for false invoicing', UNITE the Union News, 1st February, 2013.

[6] 'Sacked workers take to streets', *Fosse Way Magazine*, 9th May, 2008.

[7] 'Directors of collapsed print group disqualified for 16 years', *PrintWeek*, 30th January, 2013.

[8] Interview with Ian Leggett 23rd April, 2015.

[9] *Ibid.*

[10] Interview with Steve Burry, 13th March, 2015.

[11] Steve Burry and Matt Maiden, 'OS Maps now printed by Butler, Tanner and Dennis', *Sheetlines: The Journal of The Charles Close Society*, No. 92, December 2011, pp. 3-6.

[12] 'New Start for BT&D Maps business', *PrintWeek*, 14th August, 2014.

[13] 'Book printing blow as BT&D closure announced', *PrintWeek*, 13th May, 2014.

[14] *Ibid.*

[15] Index cards of employee records, Butler and Tanner Archive (D7690), Frome Museum, Frome, Somerset.

[16] Interview with Sally and David Bowden and Jean Hicks, 13th March, 2015.

Glossary

Beam engine A type of steam engine where a pivoted overhead beam is used to apply the force from a vertical piston to a vertical connecting rod.

Block printing A technique for printing using the raised surface of hand engraved wood or linoleum.

Case binding The traditional process of making hard cover books.

Casing-in The process of attaching a hard cover case to a book block.

Collotype A process for making prints from a sheet of light-sensitive gelatine exposed photographically to the image without using a screen.

Colophon A printer or publisher's emblem or imprint, usually on the title page of a book.

Compositor A person who sets and corrects type and assembles text and illustrations for printing.

Cylinder press See rotary press.

Die Tool used to cut shapes or impress patterns in other materials. Traditionally used for hot stamping to apply foil and emboss paper.

Drum cylinder press See rotary press.

Electrotyping The process of copying an image by the electrolytic deposition of copper on a mould.

Em A typographical unit equal to the specified point size (e.g. a 10 point font has an em value of 10 points). Traditionally an em represented the width of an uppercase letter M.

Embossing A machine die stamping process that leaves a raised impression on a book cover.

En A typographical unit, half of the width of an em. Traditionally an en represented the width of an uppercase letter N.

Flat-bed A printing press where the type is carried on a flat bed under a cylinder that holds paper and rolls over the type.

Folding machine A machine that folds printed paper sheets into signatures.

Forme A body of type secured in a chase for printing.

Four-colour process Combining the four process colours of cyan, magenta, yellow and black (also known as the 'key' as in CMYK)to create a printed full colour picture.

Hot-metal typesetting The method of typesetting text in letterpress printing. It involves the injection of molten type metal into a mould that has the shape of one or more glyphs.

Letterpress A method of printing where ink is applied to a raised surface, comprising reversed words or images, and pressed onto the paper to give a positive representation.

Linotype A composing machine producing lines of words as single strips of metal.

Lithography A printing process whereby a flat surface is treated so as to repel the ink except for the areas required to be printed.

Make ready All processes done on a press, such as ensuring the correct colours, placement of images, setting up plates, preparing printer for correct paper size and weight, to prepare for the final print job.

Monotype A typesetting machine which casts type in metal, one character at a time. The system uses a set of two machines, the Monotype keyboard and the Monotype caster.

Offset A printing technique in which the inked image is transferred from a plate to a rubber blanket, then to the printing surface.

Perfect binding The process of binding individual sheets directly to the inside spine of a softcover.

Perfector A press capable of printing both sides of the paper in a single operation.

Photo-composition A method of typesetting by exposing type characters onto photographic film or photosensitive paper to make printing plates.

Photogravure An image produced from a photographic negative transferred to a metal plate and etched.

Photo offset Offset printing using plates made photographically.

Pi-mat Matrices of pi fonts (typefaces representing symbols).

Platen A flat metal plate used in letterpress printing to leave an inked impression on the paper.

Quad demy A paper size (35 inches by 45 inches).

Ream Five hundred sheets of paper.

Rotary press A printing machine where the printing surface plates are curved around a cylinder.

Sewing Stitching folded or loose pages together along the binding edge. Traditionally used for hardback books.

Spine A book's bound edge.

Stereotype A solid plate of type metal, cast from a papier-mâché or plaster mould taken from the surface of a forme of type, used for printing.

Teleprinter A device for transmitting telegraph messages as they are keyed, and for printing messages received.

Appendices

Appendix One

This listing includes the names of publishers for whom it is known Butler and Tanner printed books. It is not exhaustive and omissions are inevitable.

George Allen & Unwin Ltd

Edward Arnold (Publishers) Ltd

The Authors Co-operative Publishing Co.

The Automobile Association

Dr Barnardo

Darton, Longman & Todd Ltd

BBC Books

George Bell

Geoffrey Bles Ltd

The Bodley Head

British Gospel Book Association

Business Dictionaries Ltd

Cassell & Co. Ltd

Chapman & Hall Ltd

Chatto and Windus Ltd

Constable and Co. Ltd.

Collins

Crosby Lockwood & Son Ltd

English Universities Press Ltd

The Epworth Press Ltd

Samuel French Ltd

W. & G. Foyle Ltd

Great Western Railway

Hachette Books

Hamish Hamilton Ltd

HarperCollins

George G. Harrap & Co. Ltd

H.M. Stationery Office

William Heinemann Ltd

Herbert, Oppenheimer, Nathan & Vandyk

The High Hill Bookshops Ltd

D.R. Hillman & Sons Ltd

Hodder & Stoughton Ltd

The Hogarth Press

Michael Joseph

Longmans Green & Co. Ltd

Manchester University Press

Methuen & Co. Ltd

The Metropolitan College Ltd

Mills & Boon Ltd

Moffat & Paige

John Murray (Publishers) Ltd

Ordnance Survey

Oxford University Press

George Newnes Ltd

James Nisbet Ltd

Pan Books

Partridge Press

Penguin Books Ltd

Rainbird McLean Ltd

Religious Tract Society

G. Routledge & Sons

Routledge & Kegan Paul Ltd

Royal Historical Society

Salvation Army (Revd. William Booth)

Martin Secker & Warburg Ltd

Shaw Publishing Co. Ltd

Society of Chemical Industry

Society of Dairy Technology

The Somerset Record Society

Sonnenschein & Co

Spitalfields Life Books

The Sunday School Union

Thornton Butterworth

The Trade and Technical Press Ltd

Ward, Lock and Co. Ltd

F. Warne & Co. Ltd

Weidenfeld & Nicolson

Appendix Two Roll of Honour Butler and Tanner Employees who served in the First World War (1914 to 1918)

TANNER, R.R.

		TANNER, H.R.	
ABRAHAM'S, G.	DAVAGE, H.	♦MILLER, A.	STARR, W.
ADLAM, H.	DAVIS, B.	MITCHELL, W.	STENT, H.
ALLARD, N.	DAVIS, E. N.	MUSSELL, P.	STENT, B. R.
APLIN, Wm. A.	DAVIS, G.		STENT, R.
APLIN, Wilfred T.	DAVIS, R.	NEWPORT, H. H.	STOLLERY, W.
AVON, C.	DURNFORD, F.	NICHOLLS, E. W. W.	STONE, H.
AYRES, P.	DYER, F.	NOBLE, E. R.	SUTTON, W.
BANE, G.	EDWARDS, L.	NORVILL, J.	
BARNES, V.	♦EDWARDS, S.	NORVILL, L.	TABER, C.
BARNES, R.		NORVILL, C.	TAYLOR, G.
BARNES, R.	FORTUNE, R.	NUTLEY, H. W.	TAYLOR, H.
BARNETT, P.	FOSTER, F.	OLDING, J.	♦THOMPSON, J. W.
BARNETT, P., Junr.	GOFF, E.		♦THOMPSON, S.
BARTER, A.	GOULTER, P.	PAGE, F.	THOMPSON, R. L.
BEACHEM, W.	GREEN, F.	PARFITT, A.	THORNE, W.
BEDFORD, W.	GUEST, A.	PEARCE, A. T.	TOPP, H.
♦BENNETT, L.	HALLETT, J.	PEARCE, W.	TUCK, P.
BENNETT, W. A.	HARLER, E.	PENNY, W.	TURK, R.
BENDY, A.	HARDING, W.	PETERS, W.	TURNER, J.
BIRD, L.	HAWKER, F.	♦PHILLIPS, F.	
BLAKE, L.	HAWKINS, H.	PHILLIPS, W.	VALLIS, C.
BOWDEN, S.	HUMPHRIES, G.	PICKFORD, R.	VAUGHAN, J.
BRAKE, W.	HUNT, E.	POPE, A. J.	WATTS, J.
BREWER, P.	JOYNT, E.	POPE, E.	WEST, P.
BUDGETT, G.		POPE, G.	WEST, R.
♦BULL, E. C. H.	KEEPING, J.	POPJOY, W.	WESTON, P.
BURGESS, H.	KNAPTON, B.	PORTCH, B.	WHATLEY, A.
BURTON, C.	KNEE, W.	PRITCHARD, R. J.	WHEELER, L.
CARPENTER, F.	KNEE, H.	RAWLINGS, W.	♦WHEELER, R.
CHAPMAN, W. G.	KNIGHT, R.	RHODES, W.	WHITE, G.
CHALKE, L.	♦LARCOMBE, A. H.	RODGERS, G. R.	♦WHITE, B.
CHIVERS, G.	LAURENCE, H.		WHITE, N. F.
CHIVERS, E.	LAY, F.	♦SAINSBURY, S.	WILCOX, E.
CLARKE, G.	LEDBURY, S.	SEALE, S.	WILKINS, F.
CLIFT, F.	LEWIS, E.	SHARLAND, H.	WILLIAMS, A.
COLEMAN, C.	LEWIS, F.	SINGER, A.	WILLIAMS, F.
COX, B.	LEWIS, Reg.	♦SINGER, L.	WILLIAMS, T.
COX, P.	LOGSDON, G.	SLADE, G.	WILTSHIRE, H.
COOMBES, W.	LUSTY, J.	SLADE, H.	WOODLANDS, P.
CREES, A.		SMITH, C. E.	WOODLANDS, R.
CRIPPS, T.	MARTIN, C. H.	SPARROW, T.	WRIGHT, E.
CROSS, R.	MILLARD, A.	STARR, G.	
CROSS, G.	♦MILLER, H.	STARR, J.	YEO, W.
		STARR, S.	YERBURY, N.

♦Killed or Died on Service

Bibliography

Publications

Adams, David L., *Frome's Fallen Heroes: the Great War*, 2000.
Carey, David, *How it Works': Printing Processes* (Loughborough: Ladybird Books Ltd) 1971.
Cuzner, S., *Cuzner's Hand Book to Froome Selwood*, Froome-Selwood, *c.* 1868.
Englander, David, *The Diary of Fred Knee*, Society for the Study of Labour History, 1977.
Fosse Way Magazine, 9th May, 2008.
Somerset Standard, Frome, Somerset. 27th April, 2006.
Gill, Derek, *Bath Street, Frome* (Derek Gill, Frome) 1992.
Harvey, W.J., *The Story of Zion Congregational Church, Frome* (Harvey & Woodland Ltd) 1918.
Hewison, Robert, *Under Siege: Literary Life in London, 1939–1945* (London: Weidenfeld & Nicolson) 1977.
Independent, The, 29th April, 2006.
Kelly's Handbook to the Titled, Landed and Official Classes, 1909.
Langford's Frome Almanack and West of England Advertiser (Frome, Somerset) 1854.
London Gazette, The, 28th May, 1895.
London Gazette, [supplement], 14th November, 1914.
Norrie, Ian (ed.), *Mumby's Publishing and Bookselling in the Twentieth Century*, 6th edn. (London: Bell & Hyman) 1982.
Printing World, 3rd July, 2003.
PrintWeek, 30th January, 2013.
PrintWeek, 13th May, 2014.
PrintWeek, 14th August, 2014.
Rhode, John, *A Hundred Years of Printing: 1795–1895* (Frome and London: Butler and Tanner Ltd) 1927.
Sheetlines: The Journal of the Charles Close Society, No. 92, December 2011.
Judith Slinn *et al.*, *History of the Monotype Corporation* (Printing Historical Society, Vanbrugh Press) 2014.
Somerset Standard, 22nd March, 1968.
Steinberg, S.H., Five Hundred Years of Printing, New edn., rev. by John Trevitt (London: The British Library and Oak Knoll Press) 1996.
Times, The, London. 4th May, 2006.
Wells Journal, 4th June, 1920, Wells, Somerset.
Working Memories: Frome Workers tell their Stories, (Frome: Home in Frome in association with Millstream Books) 2012.

Documents in the Butler and Tanner Archive, Frome Heritage Museum, Somerset

Articles of Partnership, Mr W.T. Butler and Mr Joseph Tanner, 2nd September, 1863, (DB4779/D7713/1).
Birth certificate of Joseph Tanner, (DB4774/D7829).
Flyer: The Selwood Printing Works, Frome, Sixth Annual Wayzgoose', 10th July, 1869, (DB2863/D1582).
Deeds and Conveyance documentation, (DB3098/D1801).
Memorandum of Temporary Arrangement between Mr W.T. Butler and Mr Joseph Tanner, Junior. 2nd September, 1863, (DB4779/DD7712).
Letter of Agreement, W.T. Butler and J. Tanner, 30th January, 1864, (DB4779/D7717).
Agreement between Mr William Thomas Butler and Mr Joseph Tanner on Dissolution of Partnership, 9th September, 1868, (DB4779/D7712).
Deed of Release and New Arrangement as within Partnership to be dissolved, 10th December, 1873, (DB4779/D7714).
Letter under Seal, W.T. Butler and Joseph Tanner, 15th January, 1879, (DB4774/D7771/38).
Undertakers' receipt for the estate of the late Joseph Tanner, 4th September, 1878, (DB4774/D7771/37).
Doctor's invoices for attendance to Mrs Tanner for years 1878 and 1879, (DB4774/D7771/37).

Undertakers' receipt for the Executors of the late Mrs Tanner, Christmas 1880, (DB4774/D7771/37).
Letters from William Fernie, Engineer's Office, Chicago and North Western Railway Co., 20th May, 1881 and 24th August, 1881, (DB4774/D7771/38).
Joseph Tanner, 'A Selwood Scrapbook' [unpublished notes], (DB5884/L2692).
The Selwood Printing Works, Frome, Regulations in Connection with Fire Insurance, 1887, (DB3623/D3455).
Agreement between Joseph Tanner Esq. and Messrs. Russell Robson Tanner and Lanfear Robson Tanner as to Book Debts, 13th March, 1895, (DB4779/D7715/2).
Messrs. Butler and Tanner Articles of Partnership, 30th March, 1895, (DB4779/D7713/4).
Agreement between Messrs. Edmundson's Electricity Corporation Ltd and R.R. Tanner and L.R. Tanner Esqs., 18th August, 1904, (DB4779/D7794).
Receivable: Interest, Rent; Sundries 1907 to 1922.
Deed for land at Adderwell between George Coleman Williams, Retired Builder, and Russell Robson Tanner and Lanfear Robson Tanner, 20th July, 1907, (DB3098/D1801).
Deed for land at Adderwell between Marquis of Bath and Rev. Can. Hon. Sidney Meade and Russell Robson Tanner, 25th March, 1908, (DB3098/D1801).
A short history of Butler and Tanner [article], (D8652 and DB5706).
Programme: Composing Dept. Dinner and Concert, 4th January, 1910, (DB4761/D7709).
Messrs. Butler and Tanner Supplemental Articles of Partnership, 29th April, 1911.
Will of Lanfear Robson Tanner, 16th April, 1921, (DB4779/D7721).
Notes for Managing Directors Reports to Board of Directors of Butler and Tanner Ltd, The Selwood Printing Works, Frome.
Inquest on Frederick Bishop, Coroner 16th February, 1927, (DB5862/D9789).
Receipt from Lily E. Bishop, 16th November, 1929, (DB4774).
Employee Index Cards, (D7690/2571).
Notice to employees on Butler and Tanner letterhead [undated].
Programme: Messrs. Butler and Tanner Ltd., Frome, Employees' Outing to the Thames and London, 6th July, 1929, (DB4761/D7709).
Programme: Employees' Outing to London and Brighton, 5th July, 1930, (DB4761/D7709).
Inventory: Office Furniture, Fixtures and Fittings in London Office, 11th April, 1938, Frank Colebrook and Partners, (DB5862/D9789).
Valuation figures for full insurance purposes, 26th July, 1938, (DB4774/D7832).
'In Search of Selwood: Being an Account of a Tour of the Printing Works of Messrs. Butler and Tanner', originally in *Somerset Standard*, [undated]
Letter from J. Evans & Son (Portsmouth) Ltd, Requisitioning order No. 41/W6(c), for and on behalf of the Minister of Aircraft Production, 17th March, 1941.
Letter from H.M.S.O. London, 10th January, 1942.
Valuation, Colebrook, Evans and McKenzie 23rd July, 1973, (DB5862).
Report, Butler and Tanner undertaken by Ernst & Whinney, August 1979, (DB4779/7696/3).
Valuation of Residential Properties situated in Frome and owned by Butler and Tanner, 9th July, 1981, (DB4779/7696/2).
Butler and Tanner Complete Works, Butler and Tanner, Frome, Somerset, 1990.
Letter [framed] from Delia Smith to Butler and Tanner, 13th February, 1996.
Letter [framed] from Norma Major to Butler and Tanner, 26th November, 1996.
Letter [framed] from Michael Palin to Butler and Tanner, 25th July, 1997.
Index cards of employee records, (D7690).

Company Newsletters
The Newsletter: Journal of the House of Butler & Tanner Ltd., (from 1949 to 1991)
The Butler and Tanner Group Newsletter (from 1994 to 2004)

Websites
www.historypin.org [posted by Frome Society for Local Study]
http://www.unitetheunion.org/news/formerprintbossdisqualifiedforfalseinvoicing
http://www.forgottenbooks.com/readbook_text/Alumni_Cantabrigienses_v2_1000352659/113
http://www3.christs.cam.ac.uk/boatclub/sites/default/files/WW1_records.pdfwww.historypin.org

Index